A Singing Faith

A Singing Faith

Jane Parker Huber

The Westminster Press
Philadelphia

© 1987 Jane Parker Huber

Unless otherwise noted, scripture quotations are from the Revised Standard Version of the Bible, copyrighted 1946, 1952, © 1971, 1973 by the Division of Christian Education of the National Council of the Churches of Christ in the U.S.A., and are used by permission.

Scripture quotations marked TEV are from the *Good News Bible*—Old Testament: Copyright © American Bible Society 1976; New Testament: Copyright © American Bible Society 1966, 1971, 1976.

Book design by Christine Schueler

First edition

Published by The Westminster Press®
Philadelphia, Pennsylvania

PRINTED IN THE UNITED STATES OF AMERICA
2 4 6 8 9 7 5 3 1

Library of Congress Cataloging-in-Publication Data

A singing faith.

  Hymns.
  Words by Jane Parker Huber.
  1. Hymns, English. 2. Presbyterian Church—Hymns.
I. Huber, Jane Parker, 1926–
M2130.S56 1987   86-753277
ISBN 0-664-24055-0 (pbk.)
ISBN 0-664-24056-9 (pbk. : spiral)

This book is dedicated
to our grandchildren
Kate and Peter Lowry
Gabriel Graham
Ben, Susan, and Hannah Garrison

and their mothers and fathers, aunts and uncles,
because they represent for me
in a special way
the future of
a faith that sings God's praise

Contents

Preface

Faith is meant to be sung, and hymns are for the singing of it. Some say that hymns are a greater influence on one's personal theology even than scripture or teaching or preaching or family or friends. I believe this is also true of the influence of hymns on our collective theology as part of the Judeo-Christian tradition, and especially the Reformed tradition. With psalms and chants, chorales and canons, spirituals and choruses, hymns and Appalachian folk songs, we have sung our faith. Words that are sung, especially if they are sung repeatedly and enthusiastically, work their way into our subconscious and shape us in subtle ways, as well as giving us words and phrases that come quickly to mind when we ponder or articulate our faith.

If this is true, then it matters what words we sing.

I am grateful for the singing environment in which I went from infancy through childhood to adulthood. Growing up in a high-ceilinged, many-roomed Victorian house on the campus of Hanover College in southern Indiana, we children used to sing hymns around the piano, both new ones and old family favorites. *The Hymnal,* once it was published in 1933, was our Parker family hymnbook, but we learned some folk songs and ballads, rounds and choruses, as well. And of course we went to church every Sunday, where hymns were sung with vigor in both church school and worship, though two different books were used. As a result, I learned not only "Our God, our Help in ages past" and "Joyful, joyful, we adore Thee" but also "Standing on the promises" and "I would be true."

When I say we went to church every Sunday, I mean we really went to church. There was no child care for us other than our mother, who quietly provided paper and pencil on occasion and whose hand was known to grab a restless child's knee if worshipers in nearby pews were being distracted. The first part of worship in which we could participate was the singing of hymns. Being led by the college choir for most of the year meant an unusually fine choir for a small town, and it also meant excellent congregational singing, so that singing was something we children saw as desirable from early years to adulthood.

Singing hymns has even proved useful. Later, when Bill and I had a family of our own, we peopled the choirs from "cherub" to "chancel" in church and in school for several years. On vacations we sang our way across the miles—folk songs, spirituals, rounds, canons, and camp songs as well as hymns. So even though there were eight of us packed into the station wagon with hardly a cubic inch to spare, and although there were ups and downs of moods as well as of hills, nevertheless, singing got us through the valleys as well as over the heights. Hardly a state in the U.S.A. has not heard four or five stanzas of "For the beauty of the earth" sung by Hubers of assorted ages.

Our singing confirmed for us, deep in our being, the wonder of God's creation: "Field and forest, vale and mountain, flowery meadow, flashing sea" and "For the joy of ear and eye; . . . for the mystic harmony linking sense to sound and sight."

We learned the transcendence of God: "Immortal, invisible, God only wise, in light inaccessible hid from our eyes" and "The God . . . Who was and is and is to be, and still the same!"

We learned about God's loving presence: "What Child is this? . . . This, this is Christ the King!" and "O love how deep, how broad, how high! How passing thought and fantasy!"

We learned some of the paradoxes of the Christian faith: "Make me a captive, Lord, and then I shall be free" and "Immortal Love, forever full, forever flowing free."

A legend in my family (which I may be the only one to remember since I consider myself the star!) goes like this: When I was three years old, our McAfee grandparents visited us in our new home in Hanover, Indiana. Once when we sat down to eat, I somehow was chosen to ask the blessing. (I probably demanded the floor.) However, given the opportunity, I apparently froze, and all I could say, once all heads were bowed, was "God!" in an awed tone. Grandfather McAfee was not only a professor of theology and Moderator of the church that year but a gentleman to the core, and he said, "That is the best prayer I ever heard."

I remember the story with embellishments, I suppose, but I like to think that it indicates an early interest in the language we use when thinking about God or speaking to God or being open to God's speaking to us. I confess to some uneasiness when we name God in a very folksy manner, or when we use only one idea of what God might be like. I call God, God. I like adjectives. Metaphors for God can be exciting and challenging, but if we become too attached to a particular word for God we easily become idolatrous. This is a human tendency. Too much of the Conquering King, and we find ourselves in the Crusades. Too much Supreme Judge, and we move ourselves into the district judgeships. Too much Heavenly Father, and we imagine a God who has a beard, or is absent because of "important work" most of the time, or is in the pattern of "My dad can beat up your dad!"

We could just as easily become idolatrous with a Heavenly Mother God, with all the stereotypes that could call to mind. Or we could become so enamored of a purely Spiritual Being that we would completely depersonalize God.

If we never pray except to our Dear Father, then our God is limited and we are doing the limiting. So most of my concern for language about God is to expand our understanding of who God is in relation to us, and to the whole human family—and, indeed, to the whole creation.

It may be too late to convince you, but in my growing-up years I was anything but a rabble-rouser. I was not disturbed by the clear grammatical instruction that male language could be used to include females, so I sang "O brother man, fold to thy heart thy brother" with enthusiasm, and I sang "Faith of our fathers!" with proper respect, and I certainly stood up with the rest of the congregation when we sang "Rise up, O men of God!" What happened to that docile, obedient little girl to turn her into a woman who squirms at the sound of exclusive language and who changes some of the words of hymns as she sings along with the congregation?

What happened to me is what happens to language—awareness, change, and growth, but such change often (usually!) begins with a shaking loose of one's sensitivity, a radical jolt that makes us realize what we do to people with the words we use. After such an awakening it is awkward—in fact, acutely disturbing—to read "Men will come from east and west, and from north and south, and sit at table in the kingdom of God." *People* come— young and old, women and men, of all colors, backgrounds, sizes, shapes, and abilities! That's what makes it God's table, because God is the God of all of us and invites us all to come. Is it too much to expect people to realize the genuine anguish some people experience when they feel excluded, overlooked, made invisible, rendered insignificant (even apparently in God's eyes) by language used in worship in many congregations in churches that bear Christ's name?

Early I was convinced that God is really great and powerful. The "sovereignty of God" might not have been the first way I would have thought to express this, but the idea was and is deep in my bones. Any limitation on God imposed by human beings is a real offense. More than that, it is idolatry.

The doctrine of the Trinity, which once enlarged people's understanding of God, is used by some almost as a straitjacket for God. Instead of freeing God to be whoever God wants to be, it is used as a definition, as a limitation of how we are allowed to think about God. What a far cry from the imaginative providence of the Creator God, and the table-turning liberating energy of the Redeemer God, and the mysterious unrestrained freedom of the Holy Spirit God!

When Jesus called God "Abba" (an informal name more like "Daddy" than "Father") it had the same jarring effect on those hearing it that today is felt when someone speaks of God as "Mother," or of God as having characteristics usually considered feminine. There is a shock of awareness, the realization of a dimension of God's personalness not taken into account before.

There is another factor here. I studied Hebrew for a year and am sufficiently bewildered by Greek that I have a genuine appreciation for scripture in my own language. It is important that the Book through which God still speaks to us speak in language we can understand. I was in college when the Revised Standard Version of the New Testament first was published. Heralded as "the publication of the century," it caused excitement, skepticism, anticipation. The grandfather of my husband-to-be, Grandad Priest, had been a Baptist (pronounced Babtist) preacher for thirty or forty years; he was one of the skeptics, but a friendly one. He read this new translation as we all waited nervously for his opinion. He gave it probably the most profound endorsement possible. He said, "Hmph! Says the same thing." For Grandad Priest, to whom the scripture was as integral as breathing, the particular words were not as important as the Word, which sometimes needs new words to carry the meaning.

Concern about language that truly communicates has been central to our understanding of ourselves as people of the Word, and especially as bearers of the Reformed faith. How is it that we—whose ancestors in the faith were martyred for daring to bring scripture and liturgies to the people in language they spoke and could understand—how is it that we sometimes resist growing into new forms of expression appropriate for our time and place? Are we saying that it is not important to communicate with those who are alienated by exclusive language? Is the inconvenience or temporary awkwardness that may occur in making language more inclusive more important than making an effort to include those who otherwise feel excluded? No! Which takes precedence, the self-image of the speaker or the feeling of the hearer? Lest any of us feel superior to any other, those using inclusive language can also profit by considering the feelings of those resisting change.

Perhaps the difficulty is that we too easily let our faith get set in certain modes of expression. We forget that it is a singing faith, like Bach variations on a theme, which stretch you to new understandings of tone and harmony, or like jazz improvisation, which develops even as it is being played and heard.

We are in an exciting time in church hymnody. There is great activity in Great Britain and in this country in writing hymns in the English language. And there is activity in other parts of the world less available to me because of my limitations of language. In ecumenical circles, music is increasingly recognized as a mutual bond that only needs encouragement to bring us closer together as one family of faith. But the fresh new growth is not a rejection of the past so much as a widening of the circle to make room for today's contributions. Not all current hymns will endure, of course, and we can be grateful for that. Some will live on and will enrich the treasure store of church hymnody in their own way.

So this book is not meant to be a complete hymnbook. We would be sorely limited by only one writer of hymns because of the single viewpoint and also because of the single time in history and the limited context of only one individual's life. I write happily out of my own experience, knowing that my experience is not all there is to sing or say. I have consciously tried to fill some of the gaps I see in today's hymnody, so there are several hymns that deal with themes of peacemaking and justice, liberation and vision, partnership in individual lives and in the life of the church ecumenical.

"Sticks and stones may break my bones, but words will never hurt me" is simply *not* true. Words do hurt deep inside sometimes, so that people may leave our churches weighed down by an overwhelming sense of futility and rejection. But words can also heal, and encourage, and reconcile. That is what the words in this book are intended to do: to reconcile, to build bridges, to put into contemporary words our common hopes and visions for the future so that we can sing *together,* because ours is a singing faith.

My thanks to brothers and sisters, friends and critics, inspirers and challengers, editors and proofreaders, and especially to Bill, with whom I love to sing.

Jane Parker Huber

Pentecost, 1986

Introduction:
How Do You Write a Hymn?

My interest in hymn-writing started with the planning for the 1976 National Meeting of United Presbyterian Women. The small group working on the worship–Bible-study–music–movement sequence wanted a theme hymn. The program planners had decided upon the theme "Live Into Hope." The biblical base for the meeting was to be Luke 4, but every hymn we considered had some snag for us. We were looking for inclusive language, biblically based ideas set in contemporary words and phrases, singability, a focused way of helping participants accept the theme as their own, and an exciting, worshipful blend of words and music.

All this simmered and stewed in my head as the work on the National Meeting continued on several fronts. Finally, I sat down at my typewriter and about twelve stanzas appeared—a bit much—so I whittled back to these four; the tune is "Truro" (see No. 62 in this book):

> Live into hope of captives freed,
> Of sight regained, the end of greed.
> Th'oppressed shall be the first to see
> The year of God's own jubilee!
>
> Live into hope the blind shall see
> With insight and with clarity,
> Removing shades of pride and fear—
> A vision of our God brought near.
>
> Live into hope of liberty,
> The right to speak, the right to be,
> The right to have one's daily bread,
> To hear God's word and thus be fed.
>
> Live into hope of captives freed
> From chains of fear or want or greed.
> God now proclaims our full release
> To faith and hope and joy and peace.

Reprinted from *Reformed Liturgy and Music*, vol. 18, no. 3 (Summer 1984), with permission of the Office of Worship, Presbyterian Church (U.S.A.).

In many ways the writing of that hymn still describes the way I work, and my concerns remain the same.

MY GUIDELINES

In reviewing my experience to suggest guidelines for writing hymns, I discovered almost no universal principles, so here are offered simply some tips as to *my* process.

1. Get the idea!
2. Let it simmer awhile if possible. It may be helpful to list ideas, phrases, concepts, or words to be used later.
3. Choose a tune appropriate to the theme and the mood you wish to express. I cannot speak for those who write words and music together, but as one who writes words only, the framework of a familiar hymn tune provides a valuable discipline.
4. Begin! I use a typewriter; some would prefer another tool. You may well find that the first stanzas do not remain first, or lines may be exchanged among stanzas before you are finished, but starting to put something on paper is an important step.
5. Work on it until it satisfies you, but do not hesitate to ask for critical judgment from others, even accepting advice and rewriting sometimes.
6. Sing it! If you have chosen a standard meter, try it with several different tunes. This is a good test of whether the words fit the music. An even better test is to ask someone else to sing it.

These are the practical guidelines, but the more significant factors are motivations, one's understanding of the worship of God. Here is some explanation of what matters to me.

INCLUSIVE LANGUAGE

Most hymns were written before sensitivity to exclusive language became an acknowledged issue. Rather than rewriting traditional hymns (although I do not object to that), I have chosen to write new words. My intent is to be inclusive of all persons—ages, genders, racial and ethnic backgrounds, abilities. I do not use male terms and words as if they were generic because I no longer think they are inclusive. I do not use third-person singular pronouns for God because God is neither female nor male. It is we who are made in God's image, not God in our image.

BIBLICAL REFERENCES

There are various ways in which scripture may appear in hymns. The four stanzas of the hymn "On Pentecost they gathered" (No. 38) are quite specific in referring to the second chapter of Acts. So, also, the earlier illustration of the fourth chapter of Luke in "Live into hope" (No. 62).

On the other hand, the communion hymn that follows (No. 41) brings together several references to the sacrament from various parts of the New Testament. The six stanzas are printed here with biblical passages noted in order to illustrate how explicit and how subtle such allusions may be.

We gather round the table now	
In gratitude and awe.	*1 Cor. 11:23–26*
Christ is the host, the nourishment,	*John 6*
The message without flaw.	*John 1*
In joy and solemn praise we come,	
To celebrate and sing.	*Matt. 26:26–30*
Our visions and remembrances	
Alike to Christ we bring.	
Recalling now the upper room	*Mark 14:15*
And Calvary's dark hill,	*Mark 15:22–39*
We recognize our sinfulness,	
Christ our atonement still.	
The shadowed garden where Christ prayed	
That God's own will be done	*Luke 22:42*
Reminds us that humanity	
In Christ alone is one.	*Gal. 3:28*
So now Christ's strength can feed us all	
In common daily bread.	*Mark 14:22*
We drink the life poured out and find	
Our souls and bodies fed.	*Mark 14:24*
Around this table, in this place,	
Are all named by Christ's name;	
An unseen cloud of witnesses	*Heb. 12:1*
With us the gospel claim.	

CONTEMPORARY WORDS AND THOUGHT FORMS

New ways of saying things appear generation after generation, yet they seem to creep up on us until we suddenly realize that we are frozen in some old stylized ways of speaking and writing that have either changed or lost their meaning for us. Inclusive language is only one example of this. A goal of mine is to be contemporary without being faddish.

One quality of the Christian faith is the ability to admit an omission of the past, to rediscover in scripture an idea that was there all along but has been overlooked either because of a narrow mind-set, a distorted worldview, or human sinfulness. Hymns are one way of correcting such omissions, of filling some of the gaps. Mutuality in mission, partnership, justice and love in combination, and peacemaking are themes for which very few hymns can be found. Perpetuation of such omissions occurs because people like to sing what is familiar to them. But for the average person in the pew, familiarity of melody is more important than familiarity of words, so putting new words to well-known tunes can bridge significant chasms.

A hymn is a theological statement planned primarily for corporate worship and therefore should not lead worshipers away from the central focus of worship, God. Some concepts very appropriate for sermons do not fit in hymns because a congregation is expected to sing the text as its own.

RHYME AND METER

Singability is a matter of tune selection, but also of "fit." Meter is very important in writing hymns because the author cannot always be present to illustrate how the words and music are to be sung together. For me, metrical verse is most comfortable. Today's poets are much more likely to prefer a free-flowing style of verse, frequently without rhyme; but unrhymed hymns may leave the worshiper with a feeling of incompleteness. Here are some cues for rhyming.

Rhymes do not depend only on similar vowel sounds; the final consonant should match too. "Light" rhymes with "sight/rite/flight" but not with "life." Correct rhymes can be nearly impossible when theme, theology, and inclusive language are primary concerns. "Community," "world," "ministry," and "mission" are all examples of words difficult to rhyme but expressive of desirable ideas. Keep at it; rhyme and meter are worth the effort! Here are a couple of stanzas from a hymn written for the 1982 National Meeting of United Presbyterian Women (No. 17) to be sung to the tune "Lobe den Herren." The meter and rhyme scheme are unusual and interesting:

> O God of vision far greater
>   than all human scheming,
> Gather us now in your presence,
>   refreshing, redeeming.
>   Show us anew
>   Life in your breathtaking view,
> Lovely beyond all our dreaming.
>
> Break the sun's rays into color,
>   a rainbow around us.
> Storm clouds, though real and near,
>   are not enough to confound us.
>   Arched in the sky,
>   Beauty and promise are high,
> Giving us hope to astound us.

GETTING STARTED

How does one start? Quite often ideas for new hymns are suggested to me by others who have discovered a gap in hymnody or who have a special meeting or occasion for which they would like a new hymn. That's helpful, especially if some expansion of their basic idea is also offered. People sometimes suggest a favorite tune as well, one they think would be enhanced by new words.

Usually I choose a hymn tune that suits the mood of the hymn I will be writing. That establishes a meter and indicates a possible rhyme scheme. I work with that particular tune till the words are complete. At that point, I sometimes change my mind about the tune; I like strong Welsh tunes in a minor key but am often persuaded by others that an upbeat melody will be more appealing.

The metrical index of a standard hymnal is a valuable tool for an aspiring hymn writer, and being able to change from one tune to another of the same metrical code is a great help to people as they begin to experiment with singing new hymns in worship.

By using familiar tunes, interesting arrangements for choirs can be easily made, using descants, exchanging soprano and tenor lines, or singing in unison with variation on the melody in the accompaniment.

So give it a try! Decide what is important to you in hymns: theology, inclusive language, honesty in biblical references, freshness, rhyme, meter, a particular theme, or whatever. And let all the people sing!

O God, Whom We Praise

1

1 O God, whom we praise from morn - ing till night,
2 We know with - out you our liv - ing is vain.
3 Our know - ledge is frail. Your wis - dom is pure.
4 Now fit us for life in this time and place.

Your grace fills our days as lus - trous as light.
You give us a view of life that's hu - mane,
Our schem - ing may fail. Your ac - tions are sure.
Calm all fear and strife and grant us the grace

In joy or in sor - row we call on your name,
Of grow - ing and learn - ing that nev - er should cease,
Our striv - ing can nev - er our full hopes at - tain.
To stand with our Sav - ior, pro - claim - ing to all,

To - day and to - mor - row, as al - ways the same.
Of work - ing and yearn - ing for jus - tice and peace.
Your truth last for - ev - er, e - ter - nal your reign.
By faith and be - hav - ior, re - sponse to your call.

Jane Parker Huber, 1986

HANOVER 10 10 11 11
William Croft, *Supplement to the New Version*, 1708

2   # Come and Rejoice!

1 Come and re - joice! Sing mel - o - dies of praise.
2 Come and re - joice! for Christ has made us one,
3 Come and re - joice! We cel - e - brate this day
4 Come and re - joice! north, south, and east and west!

Blend voice and col - or, har - mo - ny and light.
Though we may sing or dance a diff - erent beat.
When we can gath - er, cir - cling all the earth,
Speak out in hope that strife and war shall cease.

All crea - tures now your pure thanks - giv - ing raise
In work and wor - ship may God's will be done
Strength - ened by Christ, in whose strong name we pray,
Song, prayer, and ac - tion be our faith's true test,

To God who made both dawn and rest - ful night.
As we, in var - ied ways, our tasks com - plete.
By whose re - demp - tion we re - ceive new birth.
Her - ald the com - ing of God's reign of peace!

Jane Parker Huber, 1985

TOULON 10 10 10 10
Genevan Psalter, 1551

As Earth Turns Toward Light

3

1 As earth turns toward light, As flowers face the sun,
2 You call us to care For jus - tice and peace,
3 U - nite us in prayer On this day of days,
4 O come and re - joice To - geth - er in prayer.

From morn - ing till night We yearn toward the One:
For new ways to dare To work and not cease,
And teach us to share In un - num - bered ways.
Praise God in one voice, Good news to de - clare,

De - sign - er and Mak - er of crea - tures and sod,
Till there comes a dawn - ing that ends the dark night
Our skills, strengths, and voi - ces no pro - ject need shirk,
For Christ is vic - to - rious in con - quer - ing fear.

Of calm sea and break - er, our life - giv - ing God!
Of ap - a - thy's yawn - ing and sin's grip - ping fright.
When each heart re - joic - es in wor - ship and work.
The fu - ture is glo - rious! Sal - va - tion is here!

Jane Parker Huber, 1985

LYONS 10 10 11 11
Adapted from J. Michael Haydn (1737–1806)

4

God of History—Recent, Ancient

1 God of his-tory— re - cent, an - cient— God of
2 You have called us from di - vi - sion In - to
3 How are we, then, called to an - swer As we
4 God, you point us toward the fu - ture Where Christ

ev - ery yes - ter - day, Still our God in this day's
u - ni - ty and hope. Each and all be - long to -
work and as we live, Called to jus - tice, called to
leads and shows the way. Here and now, work not yet

mo - ments, Where we go or where we stay: You have
geth - er In the world's ka - lei - do - scope. Help us
mis - sion, Learn - ing to re - ceive and give? Shall we
fin - ished Needs our strength and will to - day. Thus we

set us in this con - text, Time, re - la - tion -
lis - ten to the voic - es Dar - ing us to
build a bridge of prom - ise? Tear down walls that
move in - to to - mor - row, Called to live and

ship,   and   place,   Hear   our   praise   and   glad   thanks -
be   and   do   What   you   plan   for   church   and
split,   di - vide?   Fling   wide   door - ways,   o - pen
work   and   be   Rec - on - cil - ers,   pil - grim

giv - ing   For   all   signs   of   pre - sent   grace.
peo - ple,   Lov - ing   oth - ers,   prais - ing   you.
win - dows?   Let   the   Spir - it   come   in - side?
peo - ple,   Called   by   Christ,   by   Christ   set   free.

Jane Parker Huber, 1984

Words © 1984 Jane Parker Huber

HYFRYDOL   87 87 D
Rowland Hugh Prichard, 1855

5   ## On Wings of Morning

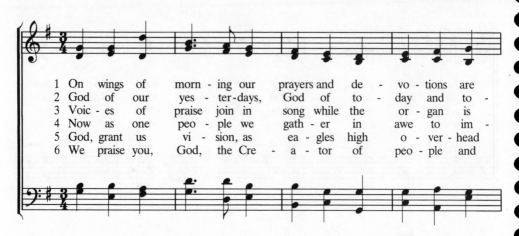

1 On wings of morn-ing our prayers and de-vo-tions are
2 God of our yes-ter-days, God of to-day and to-
3 Voic-es of praise join in song while the or-gan is
4 Now as one peo-ple we gath-er in awe to im-
5 God, grant us vi-sion, as ea-gles high o-ver-head
6 We praise you, God, the Cre-a-tor of peo-ple and

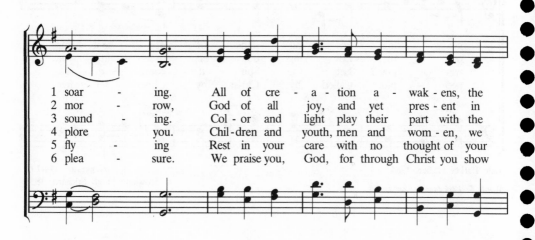

1 soar - ing. All of cre-a-tion a-wak-ens, the
2 mor - row, God of all joy, and yet pres-ent in
3 sound - ing. Col-or and light play their part with the
4 plore you. Chil-dren and youth, men and wom-en, we
5 fly - ing Rest in your care with no thought of your
6 plea - sure. We praise you, God, for through Christ you show

1 Mak-er a - dor - ing. Join in the song. Har-mo-nies
2 trou-ble or sor - row, Em-man-u-el! "God with us!"
3 mu-sic sur-round - ing. Hearts set a-fire! Art-ists our
4 here bow be-fore you. Part-ners we stand, Scat-tered or
5 pleas-ure de-fy - ing. Help us to see Clear-ly what
6 love be-yond mea - sure. Spir-it, a-bound! God-head suf-

1 blend-ing   a - long,   Vig - or and   life now re - stor   -   ing.
2 Good news   to   tell!   All earth our   glad-ness may   bor   -   row!
3 spir - its   in - spire,   Fill - ing, o'er - flow-ing, a - stound   -   ing!
4 joined hand   in   hand,   Seek-ing your   will, we a - dore   you.
5 we're called   to   be   When on your   Spir - it re - ly   -   ing.
6 fic - ient   sur - round!   Mak-ing our   life a rich   trea   -   sure.

Jane Parker Huber, 1984

Words © 1984 Jane Parker Huber

LOBE DEN HERREN   14 14 478
Stralsund Gesangbuch, 1665
Arr. in *Praxis Pietatis Melica,* 1668

6   O God of Time, Yet Timeless Too

1 O God of time, yet time - less too, And
2 We praise you now for mu - sic, art, For
3 Our hymns, ex - pres - sions of our souls, Our
4 The words we speak, the praise we sing, The
5 Our praise be - gins with morn - ing light, Con -

1 pres - ent dai - ly in our need, Our breath, our strength in
2 all en - rich - ment of our lives, For word and thought, for
3 bold - est vi - sions, in - most dreams, We of - fer all our
4 prayers our hearts may dare to raise, Ac - cept, we pray, each
5 tin - ues through the noon - day sun, And ech - oes still as

1 all we do, The bread of life on which we feed:
2 mind and heart, The root - ed depth on which life thrives.
3 cher - ished goals In trust that Christ for - gives, re - deems.
4 thought we bring In wor - ship, ad - o - ra - tion, praise.
5 shad - owed night Re - peats the song, Most Ho - ly One.

Jane Parker Huber, 1986

TALLIS' CANON LM
Thomas Tallis, c. 1567

O God of All Creation

7

1 O God of all cre - a - tion, Of sun and moon and star,
2 You call to peace and jus - tice, Yet we op - press, di - vide.
3 Cre - a - tor of this plan - et (Small speck in space and time!)

Of con - tin - ent and na - tion, Of peo - ple near and far:
Our sys - tems breed in - jus - tice. We mire in greed and pride.
No oth - er god can span it; You on - ly are sub - lime!

En - fuse us with your Spir - it, En - liv - en us, we pray.
Re - claim and re - cre - ate us For u - ni - ty and grace,
We mar - vel at your pur - pose, Your prov - i - dence and care.

O speak and make us hear it, Your word for this new day.
Dis - card - ing rank and stat - us As val - ues to em - brace.
May we re - flect your love thus To peo - ple ev - ery - where.

Jane Parker Huber, 1985

Words © 1986 Jane Parker Huber

LLANGLOFFAN 76 76 D
Daniel Evans' *Hymnau a Thonau*

8   God, You Spin the Whirling Planets

1 God, you spin the whirl-ing plan-ets, Fill the seas and
2 You have called us to be faith-ful In our life and
3 God, your word is still cre-at-ing, Call-ing us to

spread the plain, Mold the moun-tains, fash-ion blos-soms,
min-is-try. We re-spond in grate-ful wor-ship
life made new. Now re-veal to us fresh vis-tas

Call forth sun-shine, wind, and rain. We, cre-a-ted in your
Joined in one com-mu-ni-ty. When we blur your gra-cious
Where there's work to dare and do. Keep us clear of all dis-

im-age, Would a true re-flec-tion be Of your jus-tice,
im-age, Fo-cus us and make us whole. Healed and strength-ened
tor-tion. Pol-ish us with lov-ing care. Thus, new crea-tures

grace, and mer - cy   And   the   truth   that   makes us   free.
as   your peo - ple,   We   move   on - ward   toward your   goal.
in   your im - age,   We'll pro - claim   Christ   ev - ery - where.

Jane Parker Huber, 1978

AUSTRIAN HYMN   87 87 D
Franz Joseph Haydn, 1797

Words © 1980 Jane Parker Huber

Creator God, Creating Still   9

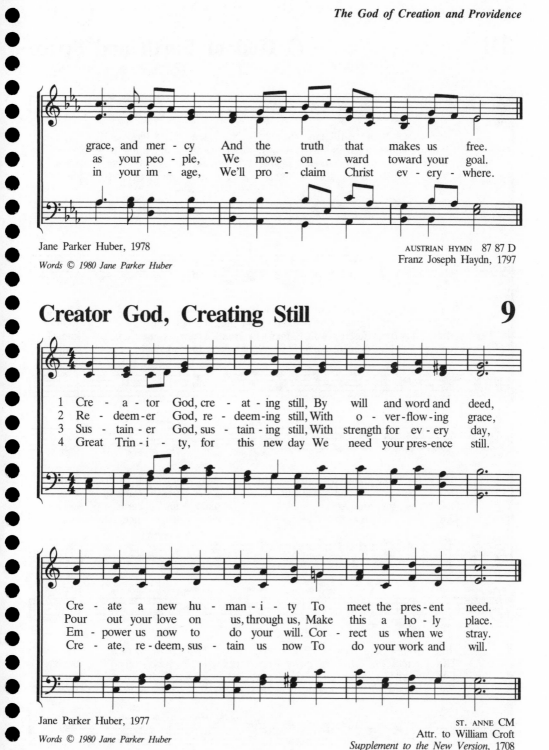

1 Cre - a - tor God, cre - at - ing still, By   will   and word and   deed,
2 Re - deem - er God, re - deem - ing still, With   o - ver - flow - ing   grace,
3 Sus - tain - er God, sus - tain - ing still, With   strength for ev - ery   day,
4 Great Trin - i - ty,   for   this new day We   need your pres - ence   still.

Cre - ate   a   new hu - man - i - ty To   meet the pres - ent   need.
Pour   out your love   on   us, through us, Make   this   a   ho - ly   place.
Em - power us   now   to   do your will. Cor - rect   us when we   stray.
Cre - ate,   re - deem, sus - tain   us   now To   do your work and   will.

Jane Parker Huber, 1977

ST. ANNE CM
Attr. to William Croft
Supplement to the New Version, 1708

Words © 1980 Jane Parker Huber

10 O God of Earth and Space

1 O God of earth and space, Of sea and fire and air,
2 Where faith-ful-ness is shown, Where love and truth a-bound,
3 Wher-ev-er free-dom reigns, Where sin is o-ver-thrown,
4 Your word com-mands re-sponse And sum-mons us to life.

Your prov-i-dence sur-rounds us here And ev-ery-where.
Where beau-ty grac-es hu-man life, There you are found.
Where jus-tice fused with mer-cy rules, There you are known.
We fol-low, strength-ened by your grace, In calm or strife.

In fruit and grain and tree, In shel-ter from the cold,
In-spir-er of all thought! Cre-a-tive force of art!
Give us the cour-age clear To make the earth a home
Our ev-er-pres-ent help, Our chal-lenge and our prod,

In cool-ing breez-es, flow-ing wells, Now as of old.
The mel-o-dy on ev-ery tongue, In ev-ery heart!
For all to live in har-mo-ny In Christ's sha-lom.
We praise you now and to life's end, E-ter-nal God.

Jane Parker Huber, 1980

Words © 1980 Jane Parker Huber

YIGDAL (LEONI) 66 84 D
Adapted from a Hebrew melody

God Reigns O'er All the Earth! 11

1 God reigns o'er all the earth! Green hills and val-leys low, The
2 God reigns o'er hu-man life! Through youth and ag-ing years, In
3 God reigns o'er time and space! In his-tory's by-gone days, Christ's
4 God reigns! Em-man-u-el! God with us ev-ery day, In

farms and towns in golds and browns God's grace and beau-ty show.
death, in birth, in grief, in mirth, In all our hopes and fears.
faith-ful folk in rev-erence spoke To bring God earn-est praise.
all our past and to the last, Our com-fort and our stay.

God reigns o'er all the earth! Stone banks and spread-ing plains, In
God reigns o'er hu-man life! Our in-spi-ra-tion still. Through
God reigns o'er time and space! O'er gal-ax-y and sun, Through
God reigns! Em-man-u-el! Let praise to Christ be sung! God's

rain-bow hues— Reds, yel-lows, blues— Of streams and coun-try lanes.
all our schemes, in all our dreams, We see God's reign-ing will.
time-less years the cos-mos hears The heaven-ly mu-sic run.
pres-ence here makes all things dear. Let joy-ful bells be rung!

Jane Parker Huber, 1981

TERRA BEATA SMD
Franklin L. Sheppard, 1915
Harm. for *The Hymnbook*, 1955

12 Designer, Creator, Most Provident God

1 De - sign - er, Cre - a - tor, most prov - i - dent God,
2 We pray that your peo - ple will find in this place
3 The mu - sic of si - lence ca - ress - ing our ears
4 You call us to jus - tice, to free - dom and peace,

We praise you for for - ests and moun-tains and sod,
Full mea - sures, o'er - flow - ing, of love and of grace,
Re - news us in spir - it and eas - es our fears.
To work build - ing bridg - es that love may in - crease.

For life - giv - ing wa - ter in riv - er and lake,
Of chal - leng - ing thought and of nur - tur - ing care,
We lis - ten, we pon - der, we wait for your voice,
Stand with us to show us the ex - cel - lent way

For life more a - bun - dant for all the world's sake.
Of deep - en - ing friend-ships and strength-en - ing prayer.
And hear - ing, in grat - i - tude, now we re - joice.
To wel - come, un - hin - dered, your long - prom-ised day.

Jane Parker Huber, 1984

Words © 1984 Jane Parker Huber

JOANNA   11 11 11 11
Welsh hymn melody

Sing Praise and Hallelujah!

13

1 Sing praise and hal - le - lu - jah! To God who reigns su - preme,
2 Sing praise and hal - le - lu - jah! For pres - ent friends and past,
3 Sing praise and hal - le - lu - jah! Long may our wit - ness thrive,

Cre - a - tor of this plan - et And all we see or dream.
For chil - dren's voic - es sing - ing, For faith and hope that last,
For God still calls to ser - vice And keeps our faith a - live.

To - day we raise our voic - es In thanks for days and years.
For sac - ra - ments and ser - mons Through which we've known God's Word,
The fu - ture lies be - fore us With mis - sion to in - crease.

God's love and truth have led us Through all our joys and tears.
For kind - ly thoughts and ac - tions We, here, have seen and heard.
All ag - es join the cho - rus Pro - claim - ing joy and peace.

Jane Parker Huber, 1986

WEBB 76 76 D
George J. Webb, 1837

14 God of Wisdom, Truth, and Beauty

1 God of wis-dom, truth, and beau-ty, God of spir-it, fire, and soul,
2 God of dra-ma, mu-sic, danc-ing, God of sto-ry, sculp-ture, art,
3 God of at-om's small-est fea-ture, God of gal-ax-ies in space,
4 God of sci-ence, his-tory, teach-ing, God of fu-tures yet un-known,

God of or-der, love, and du-ty, God of pur-pose, plan, and goal:
God of wit, all life en-hanc-ing, God of ev-ery yearn-ing heart:
God of ev-ery liv-ing crea-ture, God of all the hu-man race:
God of hold-ing, God of reach-ing, God of power be-yond each throne:

Grant us vi-sions ev-er grow-ing, Breath of life, e-ter-nal strength,
Chal-lenge us with quests of spir-it, Truth re-vealed in myr-iad ways,
May our knowl-edge be ex-tend-ed For the whole cre-a-tion's good,
Take the frag-ments of our liv-ing. Fit us to your fin-est scheme.

Mys-tic spir-it, mov-ing, flow-ing, Fill-ing height and depth and length.
Word or song for hearts that hear it, Sketch and mod-el— forms of praise.
Hun-ger ban-ished, war-fare end-ed, All the earth a neigh-bor-hood.
Now for-giv-en and for-giv-ing, Make us free to dare and dream.

Jane Parker Huber, 1984

Words © 1984 Jane Parker Huber

HYMN TO JOY 87 87 D
Ludwig van Beethoven, 1824
Arr. by Edward Hodges (1796–1867)

Great God of All Wisdom, of Science and Art

15

1 Great God of all wisdom, of science and art,
2 Where people are starv - ing, where wars dev - as - tate,
3 Call us to a new day of prom - ise and trust
4 Cre - a - tor of vi - sions as well as of stars,

O grant us the wisdom that comes from the heart.
A fu - ture we're carv - ing of an - guish and hate.
That out - lines a new way of life that is just.
O mend our di - vi - sions and heal all our scars.

Tech - no - lo - gy, learn - ing, phi - los - o - phy, youth—
God, turn us a - round and in - vade all our lives
Call us to build brid - ges, deep cha - sms to clear,
You reign o - ver his - tory, both pres - ent and past,

All leave us still yearn - ing for your word of truth.
Till jus - tice is found and your right - eous - ness thrives.
Mark trails o - ver ridg - es of bi - as and fear.
Most chal - leng - ing mys - tery from first to the last.

Jane Parker Huber, 1984

JOANNA 11 11 11 11
Welsh hymn melody

16

Ours Is a Singing Faith!

1 Ours is a sing-ing faith! Now hear the hymns we raise, Re-
2 Ours is a sing-ing faith! Through all the ebb and flow Of
3 Ours is a sing-ing faith! Up-held by work and prayer That
4 Ours is a sing-ing faith! All thanks to God be sung By

sound-ing, strong, the years a-long, And ech-o-ing our praise.
youth and age, on his-tory's page We see saints come and go.
jus-tice, peace, and hope not cease But flour-ish ev-ery-where.
peo-ple here both far and near In ev-ery land and tongue.

Ours is a sing-ing faith! In con-fi-dence we sing: Cre-
Ours is a sing-ing faith! The mel-o-dy rolls on, Sus-
Ours is a sing-ing faith! Though grief or pain hold sway, Christ
Ours is a sing-ing faith! Let psalms and an-thems rise From

a-tion's throne is God's a-lone, So joy-ous voic-es ring.
tained by those whose voic-es rose In praise in times long gone.
still shall dwell, Em-man-u-el! God with us all the way.
sun and moon and stars in tune Till mu-sic fills the skies!

Jane Parker Huber, 1985

SANDSTONE SMD
Arthur Frackenpohl, 1986

O God of Vision

1 O God of vi - sion far great - er than all hu - man
2 Pour out your Spir - it on all now as - sem - bled be -
3 Grant to us in - sight, O God, for this time of de -
4 Break the sun's rays in - to col - or, a rain - bow a -
5 Grate - ful, we come now by Christ's in - vi - ta - tion clear -

1 schem - ing, Gath - er us now in your pres - ence, re -
2 fore you. May our di - ver - si - ty here be a
3 ci - sion. May we dream chal - leng - ing dreams of both
4 round us. Storm clouds, though real and near, are not e -
5 spo - ken. We seek the nour - ish - ment found in fruit

1 fresh - ing, re - deem - ing. Show us a - new Life in your
2 means to a - dore you. Wom - en and men, Young, old, and
3 depth and pre - ci - sion. Speak through the dark. Dis - pel by
4 nough to con - found us. Arched in the sky, Beau - ty and
5 crushed and bread bro - ken. Christ for us all! Come, let us

1 breath - tak - ing view, Love - ly be - yond all our dream - ing.
2 youth - ful a - gain, Make us as one, we im - plore you.
3 light - ning's bright spark What - ev - er clouds dim our vi - sion.
4 prom - ise are high, Giv - ing us hope to as - tound us.
5 an - swer the call, Of - fering our lives as the to - ken.

Jane Parker Huber, 1981

LOBE DEN HERREN 14 14 478
Stralsund Gesangbuch, 1665
Arr. in *Praxis Pietatis Melica*, 1668

18 O Promised One of Israel

1 O Prom-ised One of Is - ra - el By proph-ets long fore-told, We wait in ur - gen - cy and hope To see God's will un - fold. The dark of night and cold pre - dawn A - rouse our anx - ious fears.

2 In si - lent suf-fering some a - wait Your reign of jus - tice here, While oth - ers dulled by wealth and ease Can not ex - plain their fear. When proph - ets spoke and Ma - ry sang Of ta - bles o - ver - turned,

3 Cre - a - tion stands a - lert and tense To see your sov-ereign power. You choose to come a ti - ny Child Re - vealed this day and hour. O grant us pa - tience to re - ceive With - out pre - tense or pride

Help us to see the light a - head Through tri - als, doubts, and tears.
Dare we ad-mit, in trem - bling awe, Our hearts with - in us burned?
The gift of God's re - deem - ing grace: A Sav - ior by our side.

Jane Parker Huber, 1986

Words © 1986 Jane Parker Huber
Music from The English Hymnal.
Used by permission of Oxford University Press.

FOREST GREEN CMD
Traditional English melody
Coll. and arr. by
Ralph Vaughan Williams (1872–1958)

Is Every Time a Threshold Time?　　19

1 Is ev - er-y time a thresh-old time? A time of ea - ger yearn - ing?
2 Can all this dark, by can - dle spark, Be bright as noon-time glad - ness?
3 Ah yes! the prom-ised Sav - ior comes All fear and death to ban - ish,
4 So wait and pray this ho - ly day. God gives us hope to cheer us,

When One fore - told by seers of old Is com-ing or re - turn - ing?
Can shad-owed night be turned to light Dis-pel-ling earth-bound sad - ness?
And to the heart, truth to im-part, Till all de - ceit shall van - ish.
For in the Christ God's love suf - ficed; The Sav-ior's al - ways near us.

Jane Parker Huber, 1985

Words © 1986 Jane Parker Huber

LAMBETH CM
Wilhelm A. F. Schulthes, 1871

20 For Ages Women Hoped and Prayed

1 For ag-es wom-en hoped and prayed To bear th'A-noint-ed One,
2 Young Mar-y did not think to hope For mir-a-cles of birth.
3 Our hearts re-joice as Mar-y's song Be-comes our hymn of praise.

Both Is-rael's Sav-ior and the world's, The new day's shin-ing Sun.
And God chose her to be the one To make Christ's home on earth.
For Christ has come, Em-man-u-el! To claim our years and days.

Did they not know? Did they not guess What pain would then be theirs,
So Mar-y sang her heart-felt praise Of God who sets things straight;
Both pres-ent now and com-ing still, Ac-com-plished fact and dream,

If God's A-noint-ed graced their home In an-swer to their prayers?
The might-y fall, the weak are raised, The hun-gry fill their plate.
We join the song that Mar-y sings, An earth-ly, heaven-ly theme.

Jane Parker Huber, 1986

Words © 1986 Jane Parker Huber

VOX DILECTI CMD
John B. Dykes, 1868

O Word Made Flesh and Come to Dwell   21

1 O Word made flesh and come to dwell Here in our midst— E -
2 O Christ, Re - deem - er, Guide, and Friend, Our Sav - ior now and
3 God's true Re - flec - tion with - out flaw, Norm of o - be - dience
4 Of all cre - a - tion, God's best Thought! In whom God's love is

man - u - el! Now be that Word to us a - new To
to life's end, With - out your heal - ing touch we fail, Our
to God's law, In per - fect life and awe - some death You
ful - ly taught, O Christ, the liv - ing, breath - ing Word Through

chal - lenge, com - fort, and re - view Our ev - ery word and
striv - ing is to no a - vail. Em - power us now to
of - fered all new life and breath. So may we live our
whom God's voice is tru - ly heard, Speak clear - ly to us

thought and deed For ours or for an - oth - er's need.
walk the way Of truth and life with you to - day.
faith in you With joy, what - ev - er work we do.
now, we pray; Cor - rect and chal - lenge us to - day.

Jane Parker Huber, 1981

Words © 1981 Jane Parker Huber

MELITA   88 88 88
John B. Dykes, 1861

22 The Baby in a Manger Stall

1 The baby in a manger stall Is
2 We can-not keep the Sav-ior there, For
3 As God's own per-son here on earth, Christ
4 The Car-pen-ter of Gal-i-lee Must
5 So glad-ly let us sing and pray Since
6 Glo-ry to God in depth and height! Al-

1 God In-car-nate for us all, As God, true God, the
2 Christ is meant for ev-ery-where, Not just for shep-herds'
3 came to show us hu-man worth, So Je-sus can-not
4 leave his shop and home, as he Takes up the mis-sion
5 Christ is born for us each day, And Christ is risen with
6 le-lu-ia! from dawn through night! All space and time in

1 on-ly One, Is born on earth as Mar-y's Son.
2 watch-ful eyes, Nor for a wise man's val-ued prize.
3 stay a child, De-pen-dent, gen-tle, meek and mild.
4 and the pain Of life and death and life a-gain!
5 God to reign. Let earth re-peat the glad re-frain.
6 Christ re-joice, In praise to God, a sin-gle voice!

Jane Parker Huber, 1981

TALLIS' CANON LM
Thomas Tallis, c. 1567

When Christ Is Born the Cosmos Sings

1 When Christ is born the cos - mos sings. The mes - sage
2 But Christ comes not for joy a - lone To sit up -
3 The poor need food and work to do, And com - mon
4 Christ's mis - sion now is ours to share, To free and
5 To glad - den hearts, the mute shall talk. To speed good

1 comes on an - gel wings. We pause from work to
2 on some dis - tant throne. Christ now in - vades our
3 folk need jus - tice, too. The pris - oner, bound by
4 hold with e - qual care. The love of God in
5 news, the lame shall walk. Christ's com - ing brings that

1 breathe a sigh Of hope for peace as dawn draws nigh.
2 will, our deeds, To chal - lenge us to meet life's needs.
3 self or chained, Needs strength for free - dom to be gained.
4 us made plain Can ease the hurt of grief or pain.
5 lib - er - ty To be the best that we can be.

Jane Parker Huber, 1981

HERR JESU CHRIST LM
Pensum Sacrum, 1648
Harm. from *Cantionale Sacrum*, 1651

24   God, Give Us Eyes and Hearts to See

1 God, give us eyes and hearts to see   Signs   of your reign and
2 We probe your prom-is-es a - new,   As   pil-grims seek-ing
3 Each col - or, gen-der, skill, and age   Acts   out a part up-
4 So let us cel - e - brate and praise   God,   the Re-deem-er

vic - to - ry.   Al - le - lu - ia! Al - le - lu - ia!
what is true.   Al - le - lu - ia! Al - le - lu - ia!
on life's stage.   Al - le - lu - ia! Al - le - lu - ia!
of our days.   Al - le - lu - ia! Al - le - lu - ia!

So may we hear and then pro - claim   Good news in
Christ's live - ly ban-ner is un - furled   O'er all the
Our weak-ness-es re-veal Christ's strength,   Christ fills all
No power of e - vil can en - dure!   God reigns— of

Christ our Sav - ior's name.   Al - le - lu - ia! Al - le - lu - ia!
wea - ry, wait - ing world.   Al - le - lu - ia! Al - le - lu - ia!
height and breadth and length.   Al - le - lu - ia! Al - le - lu - ia!
that we can be sure!   Al - le - lu - ia! Al - le - lu - ia!

Unison

Al - le - lu - ia! Al - le - lu - ia! Al - le - lu - ia!
Al - le - lu - ia! Al - le - lu - ia! Al - le - lu - ia!
Al - le - lu - ia! Al - le - lu - ia! Al - le - lu - ia!
Al - le - lu - ia! Al - le - lu - ia! Al - le - lu - ia!

Jane Parker Huber, 1982

LASST UNS ERFREUEN 88 44 88 with Alleluias
Geistliche Kirchengesäng, Cologne, 1623
Arr. by Ralph Vaughan Williams (1872–1958)

Words © 1982 Jane Parker Huber
Music from The English Hymnal.
Used by permission of Oxford University Press.

Christ Jesus Knew a Wilderness 25

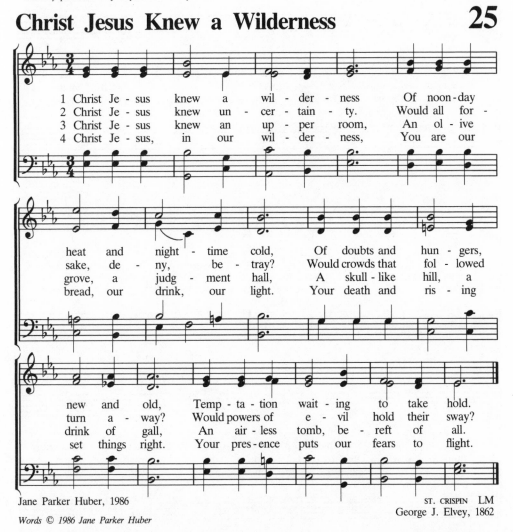

1 Christ Je - sus knew a wil - der - ness Of noon - day
2 Christ Je - sus knew un - cer - tain - ty. Would all for -
3 Christ Je - sus knew an up - per room, An ol - ive
4 Christ Je - sus, in our wil - der - ness, You are our

heat and night - time cold, Of doubts and hun - gers,
sake, de - ny, be - tray? Would crowds that fol - lowed
grove, a judg - ment hall, A skull - like hill, a
bread, our drink, our light. Your death and ris - ing

new and old, Temp - ta - tion wait - ing to take hold.
turn a - way? Would powers of e - vil hold their sway?
drink of gall, An air - less tomb, be - reft of all.
set things right. Your pres - ence puts our fears to flight.

Jane Parker Huber, 1986

ST. CRISPIN LM
George J. Elvey, 1862

Words © 1986 Jane Parker Huber

26

God, Whose Glory Reigns Eternal

Unison

1 God, whose glo - ry reigns e - ter - nal, Span-ning space as
2 In Christ's heal - ing touch and teach - ing, We see life as
3 Now we pon - der life's great mys - te - ry— Suf-fering Sav - ior,

well as time, Show us signs in seed and ker - nel—
you in - tend, Self - less love to oth - ers reach - ing,
cross en - throned, Past and fu - ture in one his - to - ry—

Life po - ten - tial, hope sub - lime. Grant us in - sight, all dis -
Pain and bro - ken - ness to end. And when hun - gry folk are
Our mor - tal - i - ty Christ owned. And as re - sur - rec-tion's

cern - ing, See - ing truth be - yond bare fact, Love trans -
nour - ished, Filled by hope and word and bread, These are
glo - ry Shines in - to the emp - ty tomb, We too

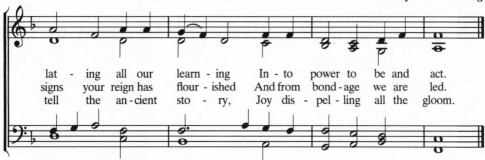

lat - ing all our learn - ing In - to power to be and act.
signs your reign has flour - ished And from bond - age we are led.
tell the an - cient sto - ry, Joy dis - pel - ling all the gloom.

Jane Parker Huber, 1982

BEACH SPRING 87 87 D
The Sacred Harp, Philadelphia, 1844

Words © 1982 Jane Parker Huber
Setting copyright © 1978 Lutheran Book of Worship. Used
by permission of Augsburg Publishing House.

As Trees from Tiny Seeds Can Grow 27

1 As trees from ti - ny seeds can grow, As yeast ex -
2 As hid - den trea - sure is re - claimed, We, God's new
3 We are not prom - ised weed - less fields. Nor are we
4 As coins, once lost, are found with joy, As Je - sus

pands the life - less dough, As light, un - ham - pered,
peo - ple, are re - named. For us the pearl, long
giv - en e - qual yields. But God's true faith - ful -
loves each girl and boy, So we, now found by

shines a - round, So does God's gra - cious love a - bound.
sought, is found. Christ is our trea - sure sure and sound.
ness shall stay With us, sup - port - ing all the way.
God, re - joice, Lift - ing in praise one heart and voice.

Jane Parker Huber, 1981

FEDERAL STREET LM
Henry K. Oliver, 1832

Words © 1981 Jane Parker Huber

28 **What Signs Has God Revealed to Us?**

1 What signs has God re - vealed to us In
2 When hun - gry folk are taught and fed, When
3 In sim - ple acts and sto - ries come The

times long past, or now and here, Signs of God's reign in
wa - ter quench - es souls and thirst, When in the dark - ness
signs of God's new day of peace, The health and whole - ness

righ - teous - ness In spite of hu - man sin and fear?
light is shed By Christ, the Last yet still the First—
of sha - lom Re - vealed when blind - ness we re - lease.

Christ tri - umph -ing o - ver death Ex - plodes the
Then faith - ful ones, re - joice, Our Ser - vant
Christ's rule in word and deed Cuts through the

pris - ons we cre - ate, Heals through the
Sav - ior here to greet! Then sing with
leth - ar - gy of the heart, Love, jus - tice

Spir - it's breath And makes the crook - ed plac - es straight.
grate - ful voice, For God's new reign will be com-plete!
we must heed Em - powered by Christ to do our part.

Jane Parker Huber, 1982

GREENSLEEVES LM with Refrain
English melody, 16th century

29 Christ Calls Us Now, as Long Ago

1 Christ calls us now, as long a-go Be - side the Gal - i - lee,
2 Christ sends us out, as long a-go Dis - ci - ples, two by two,
3 Christ walks with us, Christ dwells with us In res - ur - rec - tion power,

The call went out to com-mon folk, "Come now; come fol-low me!"
Pro - claimed sal - va - tion's hope and joy Cre - at - ing all things new.
As near as thought, as deep as breath, To bring our faith to flower.

So when we hear, re - spond, and go, We too must leave be - hind
So when we speak of God in Christ, Our grate-ful hearts a - fire,
So now may we con - vey to all The zeal - sus - tain-ing strength

The trap-pings and en - cum - branc-es Pos - sess - ing life and mind.
We pray the Ho - ly Spir - it will Our thoughts and words in - spire.
Sup - ply - ing mean-ing, depth, and goal For all life's breadth and length.

Jane Parker Huber, 1984

Words © 1984 Jane Parker Huber

ELLACOMBE CMD
Gesangbuch der Herzogl. Wirtembergischen
Katholischen Hofkapelle, 1784

Christ on the Cross Our Life Has Bought　30

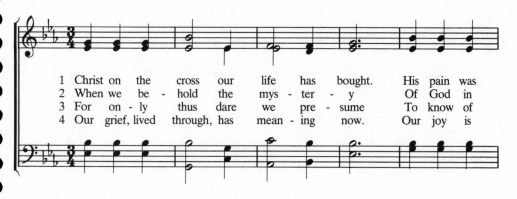

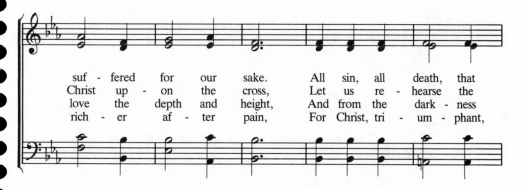

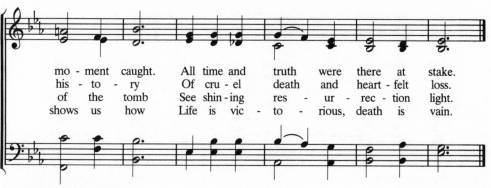

1 Christ on the cross our life has bought. His pain was suf - fered for our sake. All sin, all death, that mo - ment caught. All time and truth were there at stake.

2 When we be - hold the mys - ter - y Of God in Christ up - on the cross, Let us re - hearse the his - to - ry Of cru - el death and heart - felt loss.

3 For on - ly thus dare we pre - sume To know of love the depth and height, And from the dark - ness of the tomb See shin - ing res - ur - rec - tion light.

4 Our grief, lived through, has mean - ing now. Our joy is rich - er af - ter pain, For Christ, tri - um - phant, shows us how Life is vic - to - rious, death is vain.

Jane Parker Huber, 1981

Words © 1981 Jane Parker Huber

QUEBEC LM
Henry Baker, 1854

31

Good New Is Ours to Tell!

1 Good news is ours to tell! Let
2 Christ comes, the Prom - ised One, E -
3 Since God so loved the world, That
4 Pro - claim the gra - cious word: God

no one fail to hear! God gives us life; God
ter - nal life to bring. Though judg - ment is our
love we now must share With all whose need is
loves the whole wide earth— To lift, to save, to

con - quers death! What's left for us to fear?
just re - ward, In - stead Christ makes us sing!
as our own, Whose pain we now help bear.
rec - on - cile, To grant es - sen - tial worth!

Jane Parker Huber, 1978

FESTAL SONG SM
William H. Walter, 1894

Words © 1980 Jane Parker Huber

We Are a New Creation

32

1 We are a new cre - a - tion Of Christ, the liv - ing Word.
2 We are a new cre - a - tion Of God for this new day.
3 We are a new cre - a - tion For serv - ice here on earth.
4 We are a new cre - a - tion By God's own gra - cious hand,

Our songs of ju - bi - la - tion Shall ev - ery-where be heard.
As part-ners let us fol - low The life, the truth, the way.
We live our faith in ac - tion To tell our Sav - ior's worth.
Old bur - dens cast be - hind us, A dar - ing fu - ture planned.

New life blooms fresh and glo - rious For those who heed the call
Christ bids us work to - geth - er As col-leagues, old and young,
Let love and jus - tice blend - ing Now show for all to see
In min - is - try and mis - sion, U - nit - ed let us live,

Of Christ, who reigns vic - to - rious O'er sin and death and all.
As wom - en, men, and na - tions, God's folk of ev - ery tongue.
God's grace is nev - er - end - ing. It reach - es you and me.
In Christ a shin - ing vi - sion To God's wide world to give.

Jane Parker Huber, 1981

LANCASHIRE 76 76 D
Henry Smart, c. 1835

33 Jesus Christ, Whose Passion Claims Us

Unison

1 Je - sus Christ, whose pas - sion claims us, Call - ing us from
2 Life of life and spur of ac - tion, Christ the heart - beat
3 Light to bright - en this world's sor - rows, Break - ing through the
4 So we sing of life con - front - ing, E - ven o - ver -

age to age, By your grace, your own name names us, Mak - ing
and the breath, Keep us from each feud or fac - tion Lead - ing
dark of night, O il - lu - mine our to - mor - rows, Show us
com - ing death. All our search - ing, all our hunt - ing, Yields us

rich our her - i - tage. Sum - mon now your peo - ple wan - dering,
us to cer - tain death. We con - fess our wrong in - ten - tions.
fu - tures clear and bright. God In - car - nate, still re - deem - ing
not a sin - gle breath. On - ly Christ has won the glo - ry;

East   and west and   south and north. Shape   our ac - tion
Now   re-place them with your will. Wash   us clean of
All   re - la - tion - ships on earth, Match   our deeds to
Songs   and prais - es are un - furled Like   a ban - ner

and   our pon - dering. Meet us   here, then send us   forth.
all   pre - ten - sions. May your   grace our ac - tions   fill.
our   best dream - ing. Give our   vi - sions truth and   worth.
with   the sto - ry: Je - sus   Christ, Life of the   World!

Jane Parker Huber, 1982

LORD, REVIVE US   87 87 D
Early American

34   O Jesus Christ, Life of the Earth

1 O Jesus Christ, Life of the earth And light to every
2 O Jesus Christ, in whom we find A - bun-dant life and
3 O Jesus Christ, call us a-new To lives of firm de -
4 O Jesus Christ, best gift of God, Born, dead, and raised to

na - tion, Breathe meaning in - to death and birth, Your Spir - it,
car - ing, Grant us an o - pen heart and mind Each oth - er's
ci - sion. Give youth and age your work to do With cour-age,
save us, Friend of the pil - grim way we've trod, Let noth-ing

our sal - va - tion. Your per-fect life in ev - ery age Im -
bur - dens bear - ing. From oth-ers may we tru - ly learn What
faith, and vi - sion. Let jus-tice be the meas-uring rod Of
ill en - slave us. In u - ni-ty life o - ver-flows With

print a - fresh on his-tory's page— Life of the World, and our Life!
each can of - fer, turn by turn— Life of the World, and our Life!
our de - vo - tion to our God— Life of the Word, and our Life!
rich-ness God's good grace be - stows— Life of the World, and our Life!

Jane Parker Huber, 1982

Words © 1983 Jane Parker Huber

MIT FREUDEN ZART 87 87 887
Bohemian Brethren's *Kirchengeseng,* 1566

Christ's Word to Us
Is Like a Burning Fire

Trumpets before each stanza
(optional)

1 Christ's word to us is like a burn - ing
2 Where peo-ple long for free-dom, peace, and
3 When we are bowed by grief, de - feat, or
4 So shall the Word, still like a burn - ing

fire,   Sear - ing our hearts, our ac - tions to in - spire.
bread,   But they are giv - en chains and strife in - stead,
fear,   Warm and ig - nite the fire of faith and cheer.
fire,   Be all the truth and wis - dom we re - quire,

Burn deep with - in, O Christ, for - give and cleanse.
Grant us the flame of cour - age, light of truth.
So may we be em - powered to do the right,
Flash - ing new in - sight, mak - ing vi - sion clear,

Show us the world through God's own per - fect lens.
Use us, O God, now with the strength of youth.
Liv - ing from dark - ness in - to dawn - ing light.
Re - veal - ing Christ a - mong us now and here.

Jane Parker Huber, 1985

Words © 1986 Jane Parker Huber

NATIONAL HYMN   10 10 10 10
George William Warren, 1892

36   We Come as Kindling for the Fire

1 We come as kin-dling for the fire An-
2 Your Word is like a burn-ing light In
3 Some-times the fire is sear-ing hot. Fear
4 For-give us when we fail to light A
5 Some-times the fire burns low and gray. There

1 tic-i-pat-ing light and heat. O Ho-ly Spir-it,
2 des-ert bush, a-flame yet whole, In shade by day and
3 threat-ens to de-stroy and kill. But Christ leads on-ward,
4 lamp, a torch, a use-ful fire, But burn in-stead, to
5 are no em-bers left to glow. Can cold de-spair then

*Canon begins here

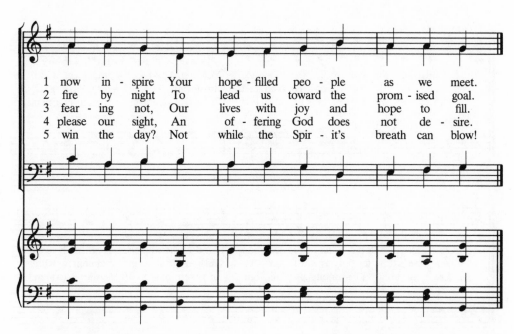

```
1  now    in - spire  Your    hope - filled  peo - ple    as    we    meet.
2  fire   by    night  To     lead   us    toward  the    prom - ised  goal.
3  fear - ing    not,   Our    lives  with   joy    and    hope   to    fill.
4  please our    sight, An     of - fering  God    does    not    de -  sire.
5  win    the    day?   Not    while  the    Spir - it's    breath can   blow!
```

6. For Pentecost still comes in power,
    Excitement, wonder, joy to bring.
  Like tongues of fire this present hour
    Enflames us here, God's praise to sing!

7. Glory to God in depth and height!
    Alleluia! from dawn through night!
  All space and time in Christ rejoice,
    In praise to God, a single voice!

Jane Parker Huber, 1985

Words © 1986 Jane Parker Huber

TALLIS' CANON LM
Thomas Tallis, c. 1567

37 Christ, of Human Life the Model

1 Christ, of hu - man   life the mod - el,   Yet em - bod - i - ment of God!
2 Me - di - a - tor   of our quar-rels,   Christ, our u - ni - ty, our goal,
3 So   may we for - ev - er fol - low   Christ, Re-deem-er, Teach-er, Friend,

Christ, all mys - tery,   all per - fec - tion,   Blend of heaven and   earth - ly sod,
As we dif - fer,   as we var - y,   Help us see the   church as whole.
Liv - ing still a - mong us, all our   Bro - ken-ness of   life to mend.

Show us how to   love   and fol - low. Teach us   how to   work and pray,
Join us now to   all   cre - a - tion, Cos - mos,   crea-tures, true sha-lom,
Thus re-born, re - claimed, re - fash-ioned, We   face   life with - out dis-may.

Grant us in our   round of liv - ing   Faith - ful - ness for   ev - ery day.
All in wor - ship   of the Mak - er   Of this   u - ni - verse, our home.
Called by Christ, by   Christ im - pas-sioned, We strive toward a   bright - er day.

Jane Parker Huber, 1981

Words © 1981 Jane Parker Huber

HYMN TO JOY 87 87 D
Ludwig van Beethoven, 1824
Arr. by Edward Hodges (1796–1867)

On Pentecost They Gathered

38

1 On Pentecost they gathered Quite early in the day,
2 The people all around them Were startled and amazed
3 God pours the Holy Spirit On all who would believe,
4 O Spirit, sent from heaven On that day long ago,

A band of Christ's disciples To worship, sing, and pray.
To understand their language, As Christ the Lord they praised.
On women, men, and children Who would God's grace receive.
Rekindle faith among us In all life's ebb and flow.

A mighty wind came blowing, Filled all the swirling air,
What universal message, What great good news was here?—
That Spirit knows no limit, Bestowing life and power.
O give us ears to listen And tongues aflame with praise,

And tongues of fire aglowing Inspired each person there.
That Christ, once dead, is risen To vanquish all our fear.
The church, formed and reforming, Responds in every hour.
So folk of every nation Glad songs of joy shall raise.

Jane Parker Huber, 1981

Words © 1981 Jane Parker Huber

MUNICH 76 76 D
Neuvermehrtes Meiningisches Gesangbuch, 1693
Harm. by Felix Mendelssohn, 1847

39   O God, You Call, Create, and Lead

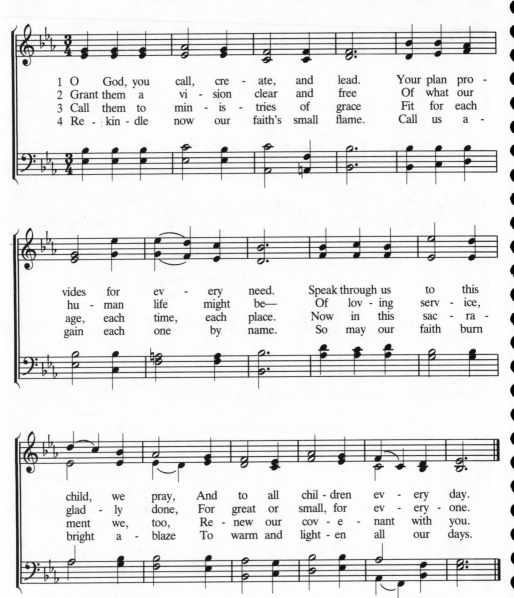

1 O God, you call, cre - ate, and lead. Your plan pro-
2 Grant them a vi - sion clear and free Of what our
3 Call them to min - is - tries of grace Fit for each
4 Re - kin - dle now our faith's small flame. Call us a-

vides for ev - ery need. Speak through us to this
hu - man life might be— Of lov - ing serv - ice,
age, each time, each place. Now in this sac - ra-
gain each one by name. So may our faith burn

child, we pray, And to all chil - dren ev - ery day.
glad - ly done, For great or small, for ev - ery - one.
ment we, too, Re - new our cov - e - nant with you.
bright a - blaze To warm and light - en all our days.

Jane Parker Huber, 1980

Words © 1980 Jane Parker Huber

MARYTON   LM
Henry Percy Smith, 1874

Wonder of Wonders, Here Revealed

40

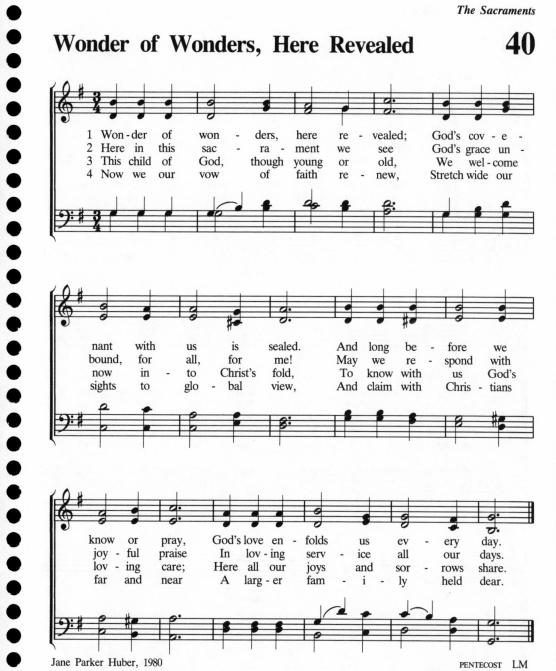

1 Won-der of won - ders, here re - vealed; God's cov-e-
2 Here in this sac - ra - ment we see God's grace un -
3 This child of God, though young or old, We wel-come
4 Now we our vow of faith re - new, Stretch wide our

nant with us is sealed. And long be - fore we
bound, for all, for me! May we re - spond with
now in - to Christ's fold, To know with us God's
sights to glo - bal view, And claim with Chris - tians

know or pray, God's love en - folds us ev - er - y day.
joy - ful praise In lov - ing serv - ice all our days.
lov - ing care; Here all our joys and sor - rows share.
far and near A larg - er fam - i - ly held dear.

Jane Parker Huber, 1980

PENTECOST LM
William Boyd, c. 1864

Words © 1980 Jane Parker Huber

41   We Gather Round the Table Now

1 We gath - er round the ta - ble now In
2 In joy and sol - emn praise we come, To
3 Re - call - ing now the up - per room And
4 The shad - owed gar - den where Christ prayed That
5 So now Christ's strength can feed us all In
6 A - round this ta - ble, in this place, Are

1 grat - i - tude and awe. Christ is the host, the
2 cel - e - brate and sing. Our vi - sions and re -
3 Cal - va - ry's dark hill, We rec - og - nize our
4 God's own will be done Re - minds us that hu -
5 com - mon dai - ly bread. We drink the life poured
6 all named by Christ's name; An un - seen cloud of

1 nour - ish - ment, The mes - sage with - out flaw.
2 mem - branc - es A - like to Christ we bring.
3 sin - ful - ness, Christ our a - tone - ment still.
4 man - i - ty In Christ a - lone is one.
5 out and find Our souls and bod - ies fed.
6 wit - ness - es With us the gos - pel claim.

Jane Parker Huber, 1982

Words © 1983 Jane Parker Huber

DUNDEE (FRENCH) CM
Scottish Psalter, 1615

Christ Is Our Unity

1 Christ is our un - i - ty. Christ is our head.
2 Christ's bod - y, cru - ci - fied, still did not end.
3 So with sol - em - ni - ty we drink and eat.

Here shall one God be praised, one Word be read.
Christ's life is live - li - est when friend loves friend.
Serv - ing our neigh - bor, our Sav - ior we meet.

And in these el - e - ments by which we're fed,
But if our quar - rel - ings those friend - ships rend,
On - ly to - geth - er may we tru - ly greet

One life poured out for us, one liv - ing bread.
Christ is the heal - ing balm all wounds to mend.
Christ ris - en glo - ri - ous, our joy com - plete.

Jane Parker Huber, 1985

CLAUDIA 10 10 10 10
A Keith Allison

43 Greeted as Saints, We So Become

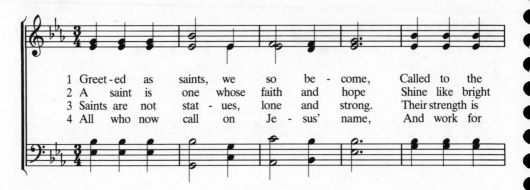

1 Greet-ed as saints, we so be - come, Called to the
2 A saint is one whose faith and hope Shine like bright
3 Saints are not stat - ues, lone and strong. Their strength is
4 All who now call on Je - sus' name, And work for

tasks God has as - signed, Dwell-ers on earth, yet
shafts dis - pel - ling fear, Lov - ing and help - ing
far be - yond their own. On earth they sing a
jus - tice, truth, and peace, God's rec - on - cil - ing

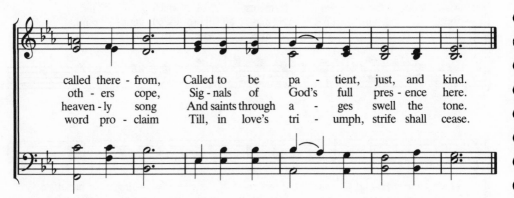

called there - from, Called to be pa - tient, just, and kind.
oth - ers cope, Sig - nals of God's full pres - ence here.
heaven - ly song And saints through a - ges swell the tone.
word pro - claim Till, in love's tri - umph, strife shall cease.

Jane Parker Huber, 1985

Words © 1986 Jane Parker Huber

QUEBEC LM
Henry Baker, 1854

God of Love and Joy and Laughter

1 God of love and joy and laugh-ter, Call-ing us to fruit-ful days,
2 When we join in cel-e-bra-tion, Grate-ful for a-bun-dant gifts,
3 Now we ask your ben-e-dic-tion— Bless-ing, chal-lenge, all in one.

May we be the ech-oes af-ter Church and peo-ple sing your praise.
Send a-gain that rev-e-la-tion Of your grace that heals all rifts.
Calm our stress, but use its fric-tion That, through us, your will be done.

Your love calls our love to be-ing, Grows, sur-rounds, up-builds, and holds,
Grant us love that's deep-er, strong-er, As the days turn in-to years,
Keep our hope as fresh as morn-ing. Keep our zeal warm as the sun.

Clears our eyes for keen-ly see-ing All the world your love en-folds.
Wis-dom full-er, pa-tience long-er, Faith and hope through joy and tears.
Keep our joy, as spring a-born-ing Cheers the hearts of ev-ery-one.

Jane Parker Huber, 1985

Words © 1986 Jane Parker Huber

HYMN TO JOY   87 87 D
Ludwig van Beethoven, 1824
Arr. by Edward Hodges (1796–1867)

45 O God of All the Years of Life

1 O God of all the years of life, From birth to
2 Through days of child-hood en-er-gy, Through youth's en-
3 May church and peo-ple heed the call To fol-low
4 In Christ, our ris-en, liv-ing Lord, We see the

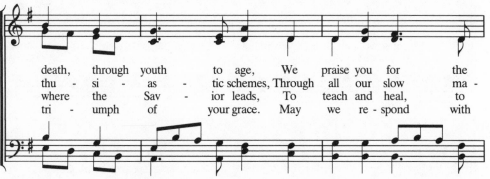

death, through youth to age, We praise you for the
thu-si-as-tic schemes, Through all our slow ma-
where the Sav-ior leads, To teach and heal, to
tri-umph of your grace. May we re-spond with

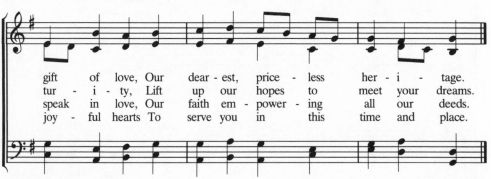

gift of love, Our dear-est, price-less her-i-tage.
tur-i-ty, Lift up our hopes to meet your dreams.
speak in love, Our faith em-power-ing all our deeds.
joy-ful hearts To serve you in this time and place.

Jane Parker Huber, 1977

WHITEWATER LM
Douglas E. Wagner, 1977

Hear the Songs of Thanks We Raise

46

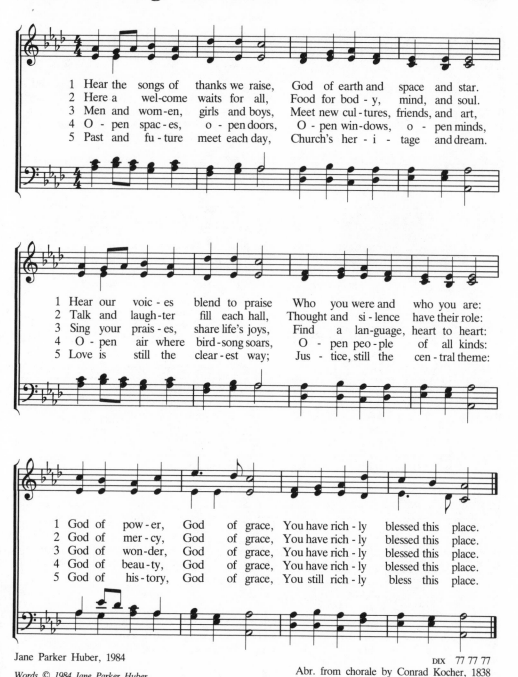

1 Hear the songs of thanks we raise, God of earth and space and star.
2 Here a wel-come waits for all, Food for bod - y, mind, and soul.
3 Men and wom-en, girls and boys, Meet new cul - tures, friends, and art,
4 O - pen spac - es, o - pen doors, O - pen win - dows, o - pen minds,
5 Past and fu - ture meet each day, Church's her - i - tage and dream.

1 Hear our voic - es blend to praise Who you were and who you are:
2 Talk and laugh - ter fill each hall, Thought and si - lence have their role:
3 Sing your prais - es, share life's joys, Find a lan - guage, heart to heart:
4 O - pen air where bird - song soars, O - pen peo - ple of all kinds:
5 Love is still the clear - est way; Jus - tice, still the cen - tral theme:

1 God of pow - er, God of grace, You have rich - ly blessed this place.
2 God of mer - cy, God of grace, You have rich - ly blessed this place.
3 God of won - der, God of grace, You have rich - ly blessed this place.
4 God of beau - ty, God of grace, You have rich - ly blessed this place.
5 God of his - tory, God of grace, You still rich - ly bless this place.

Jane Parker Huber, 1984
Words © 1984 Jane Parker Huber

DIX 77 77 77
Abr. from chorale by Conrad Kocher, 1838

God, You Have Set Us in This Time and Place

Trumpets before each stanza
(optional)

1 God, you have set us in this time and
2 We ded - i - cate this work of hu - man
3 Let doors and hearts pro - vide a wel - come
4 Call youth and age in - to these halls for
5 So may the world be - come our neigh-bor -

1 place, Called us as stew-ards of your love and grace.
2 hand; Built for your glo - ry, may it firm - ly stand.
3 here. Let walls and voic - es ring with songs of cheer.
4 praise. Then send us out for serv - ice all our days,
5 hood, Each wish-ing each the right, the true, the good,

1 O keep us faith - ful, set our souls a - fire,
2 Let truth be preached and jus - tice right - ly done.
3 Let win - dows speak of beau - ty and of light.
4 Eyes wide to see and ears pre-pared to hear
5 Word, Font, and Ta - ble call - ing us to be

1 And by your Spir - it all our work in - spire.
2 In Christ our Sav - ior make us tru - ly one.
3 Let smile and ges - ture show your love a - right.
4 Your word of peace and chal - lenge spok - en clear.
5 Bound up in Christ, in Christ set bold - ly free.

Jane Parker Huber, 1984

Words © 1984 Jane Parker Huber

NATIONAL HYMN 10 10 10 10
George William Warren, 1892

God, Creation's Great Designer

48

1 God, cre - a - tion's great de - sign - er, Ar - chi - tect and ar - ti - san,
2 Hear our thanks for those who found - ed In this place a church for praise.
3 Sing we, too, of church - es stand - ing Not a - lone in wood and stone,
4 Shape us as your con - gre - ga - tions, Called to - geth - er, sent a - far,

Dream - er, build - er, and re - fin - er— How we mar - vel at your plan.
Firm in Christ their faith was ground - ed As they lived their earth - ly days.
But in hu - man lives com - mand - ing Con - fi - dence in you a - lone.
So as peo - ple or as na - tions We can serve you where we are.

You have formed us to re - flect you, Filled us with your Spir - it's breath,
Build - ers, they, in brick and stone - work, Walls sup - port - ing roof and floors,
For high arch - es, ris - ing, yearn - ing, Soar - ing towers that fill with song,
O ac - cept the praise we bring you. Bless the work of hu - man hands.

Freed us to ac - cept, re - ject you, And, in Christ, de - feat - ed death.
Prais - ing you in all their own work— Sol - id stee - ple, o - pen doors.
Win - dows o - pened for our learn - ing— God, we praise you all day long.
Hear the hymns our voic - es sing you Ech - o - ing through years and lands.

Jane Parker Huber, 1984

NEW REFORMATION 87 87 D
J. T. Morrow, 1950

49 **Into These Hills and Valleys Long Ago**

1 In - to these hills and val - leys long a - go
2 To - day we pray for min - is - tries of car - ing:
3 Move us with con - fi - dence toward that to - mor - row

Came pi - o - neers of faith with vi - sion clear
For teach - ing chil - dren gra - cious words of truth;
For which we dare to hope through Christ the Lord,

Of farms and towns and neigh-bors liv - ing so
For help - ing all to know the joy of shar - ing
When peace and joy shall con - quer hu - man sor - row

That vil - lage, home, and church might flour - ish here.
Time, tal - ents, all; for work with age and youth;
And plow-shares van - quish gun and bomb and sword.

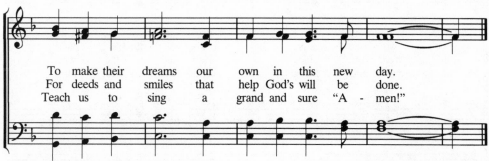

God grant such vi - sion now to us, we pray,
For wor - ship bind - ing all the church in one;
So make us one hu - man - i - ty, and then

To make their dreams our own in this new day.
For deeds and smiles that help God's will be done.
Teach us to sing a grand and sure "A - men!"

Jane Parker Huber, 1981

FINLANDIA   10 10 10 10 10 10
Jean Sibelius, 1899
Arr. for *The Hymnal,* 1933

50 We've Known Your Mercies, Lord

1 We've known your mer - cies, Lord, in times long past.
2 Long years a - go, by vi - sion and by prayer,
3 Called to the fu - ture, we see paths un - known.
4 So may our lives de - clare our Sav - ior's name,

We've known your stead - fast - ness in calm and strife.
In wil - der - ness ap - peared your church's hand,
Sound clear your voice to lead us in the way.
In church and home, in busi - ness, work, and play.

Stay by our side as long as time shall last,
Reach - ing to serve and teach good news and share
For - give our fal - tering step, un - cer - tain tone.
May words and thoughts and ac - tions loud pro - claim

And turn re - bel - lious hearts to faith - ful life.
Christ, the Re - deem - er, in this thresh - old land.
Bring us to dawn - ing of your per - fect day.
Christ, whom we love and serve from day to day.

Jane Parker Huber, 1981

Words © 1981 Jane Parker Huber

MORECAMBE 10 10 10 10
Frederick C. Atkinson, 1870

O Holy God,
Whose Gracious Power Redeems Us

51

1 O ho - ly God, whose gra - cious power re - deems us,
2 Go we to all the world as Christ com - mand - ed,
3 Spir - it di - vine, we need your lov - ing fa - vor,
4 So may we face the fu - ture with - out swerv - ing,

Make us, by faith, true stew - ards of your grace.
To be true wit - ness - es both far and near,
For we con - fess we can - not stand a - lone.
Al - ways em - powered to wit - ness to your grace,

Help us to hear and heed Christ's great com - mis - sion,
To feed the flock, to nour - ish flesh and spir - it,
May we re - ceive and give with e - qual plea - sure,
In thank - ful - ness for gifts re - ceived and giv - en,

Shar - ing good news in this our time and place.
See - ing, in sac - ra - ment, Christ's pres - ence here.
Thus build - ing up your church in flesh, not stone.
And for those mo - ments when we glimpse your face.

Jane Parker Huber, 1978

WELWYN 11 10 11 10
Alfred Scott-Gatty, 1900

52

Join Hearts and Voices

1 Join hearts and voic-es as we lift Our grat-i-tude for ev-ery gift, And mul-ti-ply each gift with praise To God who gives us all our days.

2 Our gifts, no mat-ter what their worth, We give as stew-ards here on earth. Called and em-powered by God's com-mand, We mul-ti-ply the gifts at hand.

3 All praise to Christ, the liv-ing bread By which our hun-gry souls are fed. Sal-va-tion's cup is of-fered too, As God in Christ makes all things new.

4 So may we an-swer Christ's clear call To of-fer tal-ents, trea-sures, all. God's love a-bound-ing, grace on grace, En-rich-es life in ev-ery place.

Jane Parker Huber, 1982

Words © 1982 Jane Parker Huber

DUKE STREET LM
John Hatton, d. 1793

O God, You Hear Our Every Prayer

53

1 O God, you hear our ev - ery prayer, What - e'er our land or
2 Our weak - ness is made strong in you. Our small - est gift is
3 Our part - ner - ship, sealed by our Lord, Em - powers our will this
4 So may our prayers fill ev - ery hour And nev - er, nev - er

tongue. We join with oth - ers ev - ery - where In
blessed. Our vi - sion, stretched to world - wide view, Gives
day. To - geth - er we move on - ward toward A
cease, Re - fresh - ing as a sum - mer shower To

praise of you, our gifts to share, Wher - ev - er songs are sung.
us a larg - er fam - ily too, To meet life's ev - ery test.
world re - newed, of one ac - cord, In joy - ful work and play.
bring from bud to full - est flower Your per - fect will of peace.

Jane Parker Huber, 1980

REST 86 886
Frederick C. Maker, 1887

Words © 1981 Jane Parker Huber

54 What Surging Well of Joy Is This?

1 What surg - ing well of joy is this That flows in
2 Such hope a - mid the hope - less - ness Of earth - ly
3 When in - hu - man - i - ty gives rise To death, de -
4 Those gifts of hope, of joy, of grace, Are un - de -
5 Be - cause the Giv - er of those gifts Is Love, cre -

1 dark and cold of night When reas - on yields de -
2 pain and stark de - spair Can on - ly be God's
3 struc - tion, e - vil, greed, Still shines some spark of
4 served by an - y - one, And yet they come, God's
5 at - ing ev - ery - thing, We are up - held, sus -

1 spon - den - cy And con - fi - dence gives way to fright?
2 gift to us, A gift to cher - ish and to share.
3 God's free grace Al - le - vi - at - ing hu - man need.
4 gifts di - vine, More con - stant far than earth or sun.
5 tained, re - newed. Sur - prised by hope, our hearts can sing.

Jane Parker Huber, 1983

ROCKINGHAM OLD LM
Psalmody in Miniature, 1783
Adapted by Edward Miller, 1790

Though Doubt Confronts Belief

55

1 Though doubt con-fronts be - lief, And fear has no re - lief,
2 When e - vil rules the day, Can we in con-science say,
3 Though storms may dim our view, The rain makes rain-bows, too.
4 When lives are turned a - round, When one who's lost is found,

In Christ, God gives us hope. For in the midst of dark
"We still a - bound in hope"? Yes! Pain that's ours to bear
In Christ, God gives us hope. Christ, cru - ci - fied, is raised.
Our hearts leap up in hope. Good news is here for all

Shines love's re - deem-ing spark, So we a - bound in hope.
Is eased when oth - ers care, So we a - bound in hope.
Let God be great - ly praised! We do a - bound in hope!
In mea-sures great and small. Praise God! A - bound in hope!

Jane Parker Huber, 1983

Words © 1984 Jane Parker Huber

LAUDES DOMINI   66 66 66
Joseph Barnby, 1868

56 Great God, Whose Will Is Peace

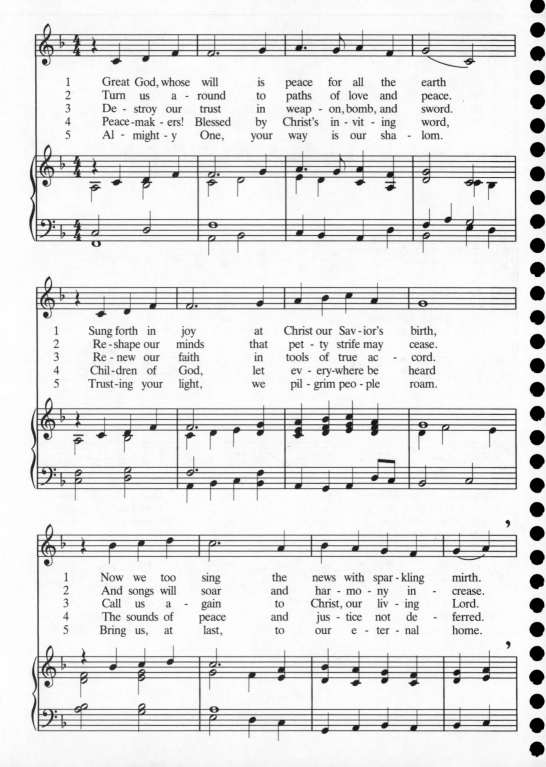

1 Great God, whose will is peace for all the earth
2 Turn us a - round to paths of love and peace.
3 De - stroy our trust in weap - on, bomb, and sword.
4 Peace-mak - ers! Blessed by Christ's in - vit - ing word,
5 Al - might - y One, your way is our sha - lom.

1 Sung forth in joy at Christ our Sav - ior's birth,
2 Re - shape our minds that pet - ty strife may cease.
3 Re - new our faith in tools of true ac - cord.
4 Chil - dren of God, let ev - ery-where be heard
5 Trust-ing your light, we pil - grim peo - ple roam.

1 Now we too sing the news with spar - kling mirth.
2 And songs will soar and har - mo - ny in - crease.
3 Call us a - gain to Christ, our liv - ing Lord.
4 The sounds of peace and jus - tice not de - ferred.
5 Bring us, at last, to our e - ter - nal home.

Al - le - lu - ia! Al - le - lu - ia!

Jane Parker Huber, 1980

WESTFIELD 10 10 10 with Alleluias
Douglas E. Wagner, 1983

Let Justice Flow Like Streams   57

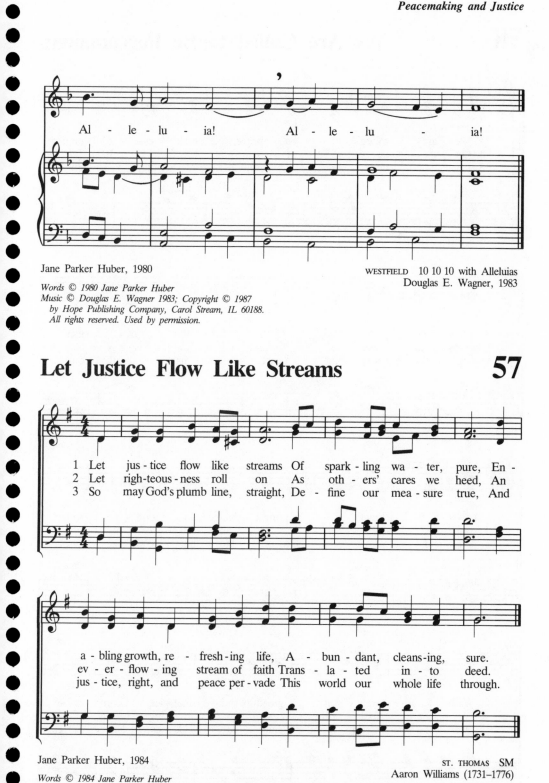

1 Let   jus - tice flow like streams Of spark - ling wa - ter, pure, En -
2 Let   righ-teous - ness roll   on As oth - ers' cares we heed, An
3 So   may God's plumb line, straight, De - fine our mea - sure true, And

a - bling growth, re - fresh-ing life, A - bun - dant, cleans-ing,   sure.
ev - er - flow - ing   stream of faith Trans - la - ted   in - to deed.
jus - tice, right, and   peace per - vade This world our whole life through.

Jane Parker Huber, 1984

ST. THOMAS SM
Aaron Williams (1731–1776)

58   We Are Called to Be Peacemakers

1 We are called to be peace - mak - ers, Chil - dren
2 On the an - vil of con - fes - sion Beat our
3 Come, re - ded - i - cate our la - bors To the

of the liv - ing God. Like the o - cean's
bombs to use - ful tools. End the age of
task of mak - ing peace. Let us sheath our

pow - er - ful break - ers, We must change this sand - y sod.
stark op - pres - sion, O, for Christ let us be fools!
guns and sa - bers; Now on life, not death, take lease.

Wash a - way all greed and mal - ice, Learn to
For the fool - ish - ness of car - ing Mocks the
Does the world scorn and de - ride us? Nev - er

live   on   plan - et   earth.   Share   the   bread   and
sys -   tems   of   this   world.   Hands   and   hearts   reach
fear,   just   take the   lead.   Christ   be -   fore   us!

share   the   chal - ice.   Born for   love,   we   have re - birth.
out   for   shar - ing,   Peace-ful ban - ners all un - furled.
Christ be - side   us!   Strength e - nough for   ev - ery   need.

Jane Parker Huber, 1980

Words © 1980 Jane Parker Huber

BLAENHAFREN   87 87 D
Traditional Welsh melody

59 The Peace of Mind That Christ Can Bring

1 The peace of mind that Christ can bring Is
2 The peace that strength - ens faith - ful souls Can -
3 So one finds peace with - in the heart When
4 So Christ, in - vade our life and will Un -

peace in know - ing how to sing In spite of doubts of
not be built on self - made goals, But rath - er comes to
each with oth - ers bears a part. When peace for me is
til we see your jus - tice still De - fin - ing best all

why or how, In spite of fears of here and now.
those who heed A call for help in time of need.
peace for you, Then Christ is pres - ent, peace is true.
hu - man worth, Re - shap - ing dreams of peace on earth.

Jane Parker Huber, 1982

Words © 1982 Jane Parker Huber

TALLIS' CANON LM
Thomas Tallis, c. 1567

O God, to Whom We Sing

60

1 O God, to whom we sing, Re-claim our lives and
2 O God of work-place and home, Cre-a-tor of sha-
3 Peace-mak-ing God of life, For-give our death-deal-ing

bring From death new birth, Till folk of ev-ery shade, As crea-tures
lom, With-in your care, As re-con-cil-ers, we Work for com-
strife. Turn us a-round! Grant us fresh grace to be, Through all e-

you have made, face fu-tures un-a-fraid. Bring peace on earth!
mu-ni-ty Wher-ev-er we may be, Your love de-clare.
ter-ni-ty, Yours for hu-man-i-ty. Let love a-bound!

Jane Parker Huber, 1982

ITALIAN HYMN (TRINITY) 664 6664
Felice de Giardini, 1769
Arr. by Robert Carwithen

61   O God of Justice, Hear Our Plea

Unison

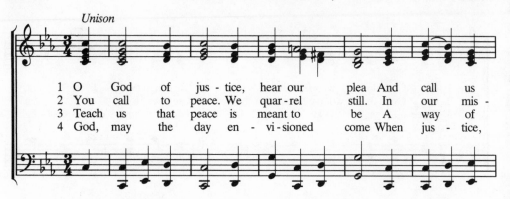

1 O God of jus - tice, hear our plea And call us
2 You call to peace. We quar - rel still. In our mis -
3 Teach us that peace is meant to be A way of
4 God, may the day en - vi - sioned come When jus - tice,

to com - mu - ni - ty. With - out your heal - ing,
trust, we fail your will. O save us in this
life for all to see, That friend and foe a -
peace, and joy for some Shall be for all, not

we are torn. Held in your love, we are re - born.
cru - cial hour, Great God of jus - tice, peace, and power.
like be shown Re - deem - ing love through us made known.
just a few, Your reign in mer - cy com - ing true.

Jane Parker Huber, 1982

DEO GRACIAS LM
English melody, 15th century

Words © 1983 Jane Parker Huber

Live Into Hope

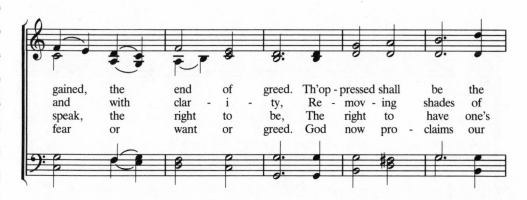

1 Live in - to hope of cap - tives freed, Of sight re -
2 Live in - to hope the blind shall see With in - sight
3 Live in - to hope of lib - er - ty, The right to
4 Live in - to hope of cap - tives freed From chains of

gained, the end of greed. Th'op - pressed shall be the
and with clar - i - ty, Re - mov - ing shades of
speak, the right to be, The right to have one's
fear or want or greed. God now pro - claims our

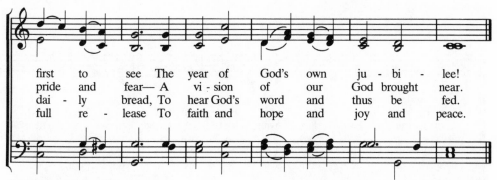

first to see The year of God's own ju - bi - lee!
pride and fear— A vi - sion of our God brought near.
dai - ly bread, To hear God's word and thus be fed.
full re - lease To faith and hope and joy and peace.

Jane Parker Huber, 1976

Words © 1980 Jane Parker Huber

TRURO LM
Thomas Williams' *Psalmodia Evangelica*, 1789

63 God of Justice, God of Mercy

1 God of jus - tice, God of mer - cy, Make us
2 How can we, as peo - ple cho - sen By your
3 You have formed us, God of rain - bows, In your
4 Grant all peo - ple work with mean - ing, Strength to
5 So the vi - sion you have plant - ed In each

1 mer - ci - ful and just! Help us see all
2 grace for serv - ice here— How en - dure an -
3 im - age for your will. See - ing our di -
4 care for those they love. Food for ta - ble,
5 hu - man mind and heart Now be - comes the

1 your cre - a - tion As from you a sa - cred trust.
2 oth - er's hard - ship with - out of - fering hope or cheer?
3 verse re - flec - tions, Trust - ing you, we mar - vel still;
4 truth for tell - ing, Chal - leng - es to rise a - bove.
5 spark of ac - tion Call - ing us to do our part.

1 And when peo - ple cry in an - guish For their
2 God, for - give us, we be - seech you, When our
3 For our col - ors, strengths, and tal - ents Show what
4 But re - mind us, God of jus - tice, This is
5 Keep that vi - sion clear be - fore us: Men and

1 own or oth - ers' pain, Show us ways to
2 love fails to em - power. Teach us how to
3 one a - lone would lack, Call - ing us to
4 now our work, our call! Chang - ing life's op -
5 wom - en, girls and boys, Val - ued in re -

1 make a dif - ference. O dear God, make us hu - mane!
2 be more faith - ful In this pres - ent cru - cial hour.
3 work to - geth - er— Brown, red, gold - en, white, and black.
4 pres - sive sys - tems In - to ones em - pow - ering all.
5 sponse and wit - ness, Shar - ing chal - leng - es and joys.

Jane Parker Huber, 1983

HYFRYDOL 87 87 D
Rowland Hugh Prichard, 1855

Words © 1983 Jane Parker Huber

64

God, Teach Us Peacemaking

Unison

1 God, teach us peace-mak-ing, jus-tice, and love.
2 God, teach us peace-mak-ing in church and home,
3 God, teach us peace-mak-ing in ev-ery role.
4 God, teach us peace-mak-ing un-to the end—

Blessed by Christ's teach-ing, we're lift-ed a-bove
In school and hall, be-neath Cap-i-tol dome,
In each re-la-tion-ship make peace our goal.
Par-ent or child, or as strang-er or friend—

All thought of ven-geance or en-vy or hate.
In shop and in-du-stry, cit-y and farm:
Yet give us in-sight that keeps us a-ware
Fill all our hearts with the power of sha-lom,

Help us, your chil-dren, sha-lom to cre-ate.
Show us the path-ways that cause no one harm.
Jus-tice and mer-cy in bal-ance to share.
Liv-ing to-geth-er, the whole world our home.

Jane Parker Huber, 1980

SLANE 10 10 9 10
Traditional Irish melody
Harm. by David Evans (1874–1948)

"Your Kingdom Come!"
Great God, We Pray

65

1 "Your king-dom come!" great God, we pray. Your
2 On earth your will be right - ly done, Your
3 May all who hun - ger now be fed, May
4 O God, for - give our pride and greed. Wash
5 In con - fi - dence we hope and pray. We

1 rule be our de - light and goal. Stretch love and jus - tice
2 law, our fo - cus and our frame, As we be - come more
3 those who thirst drink full and deep. Give us the grace to
4 clean our hearts to do your will. Stir us a - wake to
5 long to see your reign full - blown. All dis - cord past, our

1 in our day From east to west and pole to pole.
2 near - ly one With Christ, who calls us each by name.
3 share the bread And in the cup Christ's mem - ory keep.
4 hu - man need, So may our lives your plan ful - fill.
5 joy to say, "Yours is the king-dom! Yours a - lone!"

Jane Parker Huber, 1982

OLD HUNDREDTH LM
Louis Bourgeois, *Genevan Psalter*, 1551

66   Sing to Our God a Song of Cheer

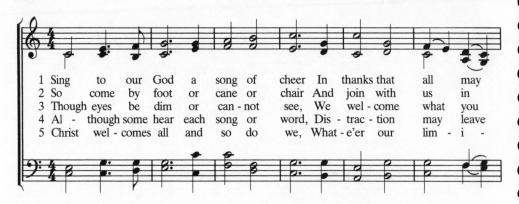

1 Sing to our God a song of cheer In thanks that all may
2 So come by foot or cane or chair And join with us in
3 Though eyes be dim or can-not see, We wel-come what you
4 Al - though some hear each song or word, Dis-trac-tion may leave
5 Christ wel-comes all and so do we, What-e'er our lim - i -

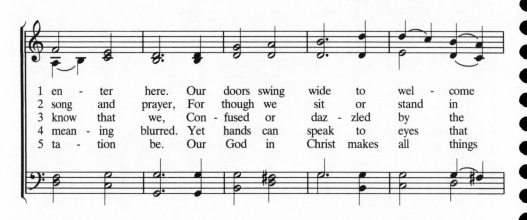

1 en - ter here. Our doors swing wide to wel - come
2 song and prayer, For though we sit or stand in
3 know that we, Con - fused or daz - zled by the
4 mean - ing blurred. Yet hands can speak to eyes that
5 ta - tion be. Our God in Christ makes all things

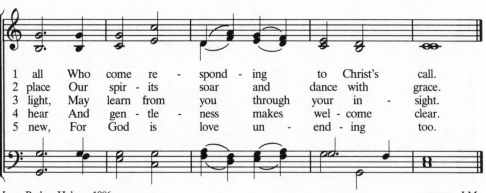

1 all Who come re - spond - ing to Christ's call.
2 place Our spir - its soar and dance with grace.
3 light, May learn from you through your in - sight.
4 hear And gen - tle - ness makes wel - come clear.
5 new, For God is love un - end - ing too.

Jane Parker Huber, 1986

TRURO LM
Thomas Williams' *Psalmodia Evangelica*, 1789

Christ's Partners All Are We

67

1 Christ's part-ners all are we, Al - le - lu - ia! A - men!
2 Sing! stew-ards of God's grace, Al - le - lu - ia! A - men!
3 Friends, join - ing hand in hand, Al - le - lu - ia! A - men!
4 God's peo - ple cel - e - brate, Al - le - lu - ia! A - men!

In mis - sion joy - ful - ly. Al - le - lu - ia! A - men!
Love con - quers time and space. Al - le - lu - ia! A - men!
Reach out from land to land. Al - le - lu - ia! A - men!
For our Lord God is great. Al - le - lu - ia! A - men!

We dare not stand a - lone, Of - fering for bread a stone,
Glad - ly re - ceive and give Strength that we all may live;
Our cir - cle comes full round. Sing we with live - ly sound.
Now serve and teach and heal, God's jus - tice to make real.

Safe - guard-ing but our own. Al - le - lu - ia! A - men!
Wrongs, each to each, for - give. Al - le - lu - ia! A - men!
Feet, danc - ing, tap the ground. Al - le - lu - ia! A - men!
All praise with joy - ful zeal. Al - le - lu - ia! A - men!

Jane Parker Huber, 1980

Words © 1980 Jane Parker Huber
Music from the Revised Church Hymnary 1927. *Used*
by permission of Oxford University Press

MADRID 66 66 D
Spanish folk tune
Harm. by David Evans (1874–1948)

68 Called as Partners in Christ's Service

1 Called as part - ners in Christ's serv - ice, Called to min - is -
2 Christ's ex - am - ple, Christ's in - spir - ing, Christ's clear call to
3 Thus new pat - terns for Christ's mis - sion, In a small or
4 So God grant us for to - mor - row Ways to or - der

tries of grace, We re - spond with deep com - mit - ment Fresh new
work and worth, Let us fol - low, nev - er fal - tering, Rec - on -
glob - al sense, Help us bear each oth - er's bur - dens, Break - ing
hu - man life That sur - round each per - son's sor - row With a

lines of faith to trace. May we learn the art of shar - ing,
cil - ing folk on earth. Men and wom - en, rich - er, poor - er,
down each wall or fence. Words of com - fort, words of vi - sion,
calm that con - quers strife. Make us part - ners in our liv - ing,

Side by side and friend with friend, E - qual part - ners
All God's peo - ple, young and old, Blend - ing hu - man
Words of chal - lenge, said with care, Bring new power and
Our com - pas - sion to in - crease, Mes - sen - gers of

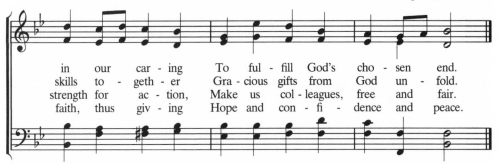

in   our   car - ing   To ful - fill God's   cho - sen   end.
skills to - geth - er   Gra - cious gifts from   God   un - fold.
strength for   ac - tion,   Make us   col - leagues,   free   and   fair.
faith, thus giv - ing   Hope and con - fi - dence and   peace.

Jane Parker Huber, 1981

BEECHER   87 87 D
John Zundel, 1870

Words © 1981 Jane Parker Huber

O God, Whose Glory Shines Afar   69

1 O   God, whose glo - ry   shines a - far,   Bright - er than
2 Great God, your will is   true sha - lom.   You make this
3 Where there are pris - ons   of the   soul,   Where hun - ger
4 O   God, whose glo - ry   fills all   space,   Yet pres - ent

gal - ax - y   or   star,   We too, your   crea - tures,
u - ni - verse   our   home.   So may we   live,   your
takes in   hu - man   toll,   Where free-dom's   song   may
in   this   time and   place,   With live - ly   praise   we

bright - ly   raise   In joy - ful   song   our Mak - er's   praise.
love   pro - claim,   And work for   jus - tice   in your   name.
still   be   banned,   There we with   Christ   in strength shall   stand.
now   a - dore   As in the   past   and ev - er - more.

Jane Parker Huber, 1981

DUKE STREET   LM
John Hatton, d. 1793

Words © 1982 Jane Parker Huber

70

The Call to Be God's People

1 The call to be God's peo - ple is new in ev - ery age,
2 We dare be - cause Christ claims us and gives us work and skill
3 So let us join to - geth - er, as God's new peo - ple here,

Yet writ - ten clear - ly, bold - ly, on all our his - tory's page.
To make our wit - ness dai - ly, re - spon - ding to God's will.
In part - ner - ship and mis - sion, be - cause the call is clear.

How dare we claim that call - ing with seers and com - mon folk
The task is placed be - fore us in dreams to be made real.
The world a - waits the dawn - ing of that long - prom - ised day

Who stood for faith in ac - tion and lis - tened when God spoke?
We find our com - mon call - ing to teach, sup - port, and heal.
When love shall be the stan - dard that none can take a - way.

Jane Parker Huber, 1983

Words © 1984 Jane Parker Huber

MUNICH 76 76 D
Neuvermehrtes Meiningisches Gesangbuch, 1693
Harm. by Felix Mendelssohn, 1847

Called by Christ to Love Each Other

71

1 Called by Christ to love each oth-er, Called by Christ to seek the lost,
2 Called by Christ to be a wit-ness, Called by Christ for this, our day,
3 Called by Christ to be earth's leav-en, Called by Christ to shed God's light,
4 Called by Christ as friends and learn-ers, Called by Christ for peace on earth,

May we each, as sis-ter, broth-er, Fol-low Christ, not count-ing cost.
In Christ's strength we have our fit-ness, Work to do and words to say.
May we bring a view of heav-en To this world's de-spair-ing plight.
In this world as Christ's so-journ-ers We re-ceive new power, new birth.

One in dar-ing, one in shar-ing, Fol-low Christ, not count-ing cost.
On Christ lean-ing, find life's mean-ing, Work to do and words to say.
Christ re-veal-ing, won-drous heal-ing To this world's de-spair-ing plight.
As we're prais-ing (how a-maz-ing!) We re-ceive new power, new birth.

One in dar-ing, one in shar-ing, Fol-low Christ, not count-ing cost.
On Christ lean-ing, find life's mean-ing, Work to do and words to say.
Christ re-veal-ing, won-drous heal-ing To this world's de-spair-ing plight.
As we're prais-ing (how a-maz-ing!) We re-ceive new power, new birth.

Jane Parker Huber, 1980

Words © 1980 Jane Parker Huber

VESPER HYMN 87 87 D
Attr. to Dimitri S. Bortniansky (1751–1825)
Arr. by John A. Stevenson, 1818

72   **Christ Has Called Us to New Visions**

1 Christ has called us to new vi-sions Here to cel - e -
2 As we lis-ten to each oth - er, As we speak in
3 All cre - a - tion strug-gles, yearn-ing For a time of
4 Christ still calls us, young and ag - ing, Men and wom - en,

brate and praise, Here con - fess our old di - vi-sions,
joy and pain, We be - come as sis - ter, bro - ther,
true sha - lom. Are we try - ing, Are we learn-ing
bound and free, Col - ors, tal - ents, thoughts en - gag - ing,

Here our peace pe - ti - tions raise. Come re - pen-tant, come for -
Rec - on - ciled, at one a - gain. On - ly thus in work and
Now to make the earth our home? For the hun-gry and de -
Joined in one com - mu - ni - ty. Christ re - mold-ing, heal-ing,

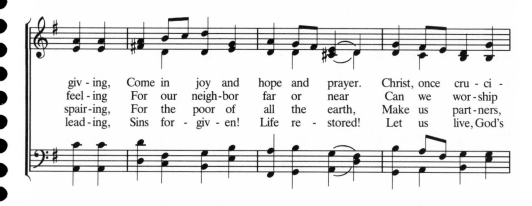

giv - ing,   Come in   joy and   hope and   prayer.   Christ, once   cru - ci -
feel - ing   For our   neigh-bor   far or   near   Can we   wor - ship
spair - ing,   For the   poor of   all the   earth,   Make us   part - ners,
lead - ing,   Sins for - giv - en!   Life re - stored!   Let us   live, God's

fied,   now   liv - ing,   Bids us   faith and   love to   share.
God re - veal - ing   Gifts of   grace a - mong us   here.
bur - dens   shar - ing,   Bring - ing   all a   sense of   worth.
jus - tice   heed - ing,   Strength-ened   by our   ris - en   Lord.

Jane Parker Huber, 1981

IN BABILONE 87 87 D
Traditional Dutch melody
Arr. by Julius Röntgen

73

Great Creator God, You Call Us

1 Great Cre - a - tor God, you call us Through the church to
2 Out of all our var - ied sto - ries May we weave a
3 Christ still calls to peace and jus - tice, Health and whole - ness,
4 With - out vi - sion, peo - ple per - ish, With - out chal - lenge,

do your will. Stew - ards of both past and prom - ise,
sin - gle tale. Here con - fess - ing sin and dis - cord,
love and grace. We are part - ners in that mis - sion
drift and die. Give us then the tools of dar - ing

May we each our work ful - fill, Build - ing up in
Times we stum - ble, times we fail. Yet, for - giv - en,
For this time and in this place. O God, grant us
And the clar - i - ty of eye For cre - a - ting

faith and nur - ture Christ's own mis - sion, live - ly still.
cleansed, re - fash - ioned, In Christ's strength shall we pre - vail.
sense and cour - age In the dai - ly tasks we face.
in the pres - ent Vi - sions far and wide and high.

Jane Parker Huber, 1985

Words © 1986 Jane Parker Huber

REGENT SQUARE 87 87 87
Henry Smart, 1867

Commentary on the Hymns

PRAISE AND ADORATION

(1) O God, Whom We Praise

The Hanover Presbyterian Church is the church in which I was baptized, confirmed my baptismal vows, and was married. There, my husband, Bill, was ordained to the ministry of word and sacrament.

The first Sunday after my family moved to Hanover, we Parkers went to church as always. Professor Huber, Bill's father, who was then superintendent of the Sunday school, carried me into the church that first day, I've been told. Two weeks later his sudden death shocked the college and community, and his replacement was my father's first faculty appointment as President of Hanover College.

Bill and I grew up in that nurturing blend of church and town, college and countryside. There is a stone marker in the churchyard commemorating the founding of the Presbyterian seminary that later became McCormick Theological Seminary in Chicago, where we spent challenging and happy seminary years. Our first two children were born during those seminary years, and the eldest was baptized by her grandfather in the Hanover Presbyterian Church.

It is easy to be sentimental about Hanover, our childhood home and our college. However, the Hanover church is not a sentimental church. It is a congregation of caring, thinking, singing, working, faithful people. I was reminded, when asked to consider writing a hymn for them, that they did not want an alma mater; it should be a hymn. And here it is. My concession to sentiment was to choose the tune "Hanover."

(2) Come and Rejoice!
(3) As Earth Turns Toward Light

These two hymns were written for the centennial celebration of the World Day of Prayer, a special service of worship sponsored by the International Committee for World Day of Prayer and held in the Riverside Church, New

York City, on May 18, 1986, Pentecost Sunday. This commemorative service anticipated the worldwide services to be held on March 6, 1987. Both hymns speak of the whole people of God, praying and working for justice and peace in the world community.

"Come and rejoice" appears here set to the tune "Toulon." When it was sung for the centennial celebration, the tune "National Hymn" was used.

"Informed Prayer" and "Prayerful Action" are the keys to World Day of Prayer, a global movement celebrated annually on the first Friday of March. Prayers begin in the Pacific Islands at the dateline and move westward with the sun. These hymns, although written with a particular kind of prayer service in mind, are applicable to all worship in a global context, as Christian worship ideally is.

To add a personal note: our granddaughter Hannah Rebekah Garrison was born on May 18, 1986, the day "Come and rejoice" was first sung in the centennial celebration, so on that Pentecost Sunday she was welcomed into the worldwide household of faith with great rejoicing.

(4) God of History—Recent, Ancient
John 17:21–24; Ephesians 2:14; Micah 6:8

This hymn was written for "Today Into Tomorrow: A Year of Consultations, 1984–1985," in the newly reunited Presbyterian Church (U.S.A.). The General Assembly Council initiated the process of consultations at the direction of the reuniting General Assembly to provide the basis for a new design for carrying out the mission of the church. As a member of the Council's Mission Design Committee, I was involved in working on the initial presentation of the year of consultations to the 1984 General Assembly in Phoenix. The hymn was written at the suggestion of the committee for use in combination with a multimedia piece highlighting the church's mission and ministry, its diversity of age, race, gender, culture, and skills, and its hopes for the future.

The first tune suggested to me, before I started writing, was "Nettleton" ("Come, Thou Fount of every blessing"), but in the end "Hyfrydol" was chosen. I like either one.

(5) On Wings of Morning

A request from First Presbyterian Church, Birmingham, Michigan, came for a sesquicentennial hymn for their 150th anniversary in 1984. As it happened, I was in Detroit Presbytery for a meeting several months before their celebration and had time to visit the church briefly before catching my flight home. That visit, in addition to several flyers, newsletters, worship bulletins, and brochures about the congregation and its activities, provided the content for this hymn.

Art in various forms appears in the hymn: stained-glass windows, sculpture, music of instruments and voices. But underneath all is the recognition that people in praise of God are what makes a church strong and vital. A sense of partnership and a special international program called "Hand in Hand" also are mentioned, but not in such a way as to limit the use of the hymn exclusively to this congregation.

The long, flowing line of the tune "Lobe den Herren," alternately with its shorter internal lines, enhances the piece. Six stanzas are a few too many for most occasions, but there were several ideas to incorporate for the particular celebration. For regular use some stanzas could be omitted. Another interesting possibility might be to use the first four stanzas as an opening hymn of praise and the last two in commitment and gratitude at the end of the service.

(6) O God of Time, Yet Timeless Too

When the request came to me from the Art Committee of Tabernacle Presbyterian Church, Indianapolis, for a special hymn for the dedication of their organ, several hymn tunes were suggested that would lend themselves to variations, choir arrangements, and combined choir and congregation settings. Also, it was clear that a hymn of praise was desired that would be useful for other worship services. In this hymn, the middle three stanzas focus on particular forms of worship common to many occasions; the first and last stanzas could stand alone as a shorter hymn or perhaps as an introit or benediction response.

"Tallis' Canon" is a favorite of mine, partly because of the strong, singable line in an easy range, and partly because it is a canon or round. Singing it in canon provides a quiet beginning, building to a climax and tapering off to a thoughtful ending. I like to write the end of the final stanza, the last four syllables, with that possibility in mind. Thus, here the ending is "Most Holy One." That is a fitting note of awe before the God whom we worship.

(7) O God of All Creation

A request came from the Arkansas Conference of Churches and Synagogues for a new hymn to express our praise of the One God and our commitment to work together for peace and justice. Because the Arkansas Conference includes Jews as well as Christians, this is an even wider ecumenical context than usual.

My preference for a melody is "Llangloffan," a firm, compelling Welsh tune in a minor key. However, "Llangloffan" is not as familiar as "Lancashire," so, especially if words are to be printed without the music or sung without rehearsal, "Lancashire" (see No. 32 in this book) may be the surer choice.

(8) God, You Spin the Whirling Planets
Genesis 1; 1 Corinthians 5:17

"In the Image of God" was the announced theme of the 1979 National Meeting of United Presbyterian Women. The story of creation, especially Genesis 1:26–27, was to be the biblical focus, and I was told that the planning committee was looking at various ways in which we use the concept of "image" and what that says about human beings being made "in the image of God." The three stanzas of this hymn pick up several facets of the idea of image: reflection, focus, distortion, polishing to make the image clearer.

The hymn originally appeared in a booklet compiled for that UPW meeting by Ann Lodge. The hymn was named "In God's Image" and appeared as the first one in the song booklet titled *Creation Sings.*

Opening night at the meeting was to feature a presentation of *Haydn's Creation,* so it seemed singularly appropriate to use Haydn's "Austrian Hymn" as the tune for this theme hymn. (Some people have told me they prefer "Hyfrydol" or "In Babilone," since Haydn's tune [with "Deutschland über Alles"] was sung so frequently in Nazi Germany.) A particularly thrilling moment for me came later in the meeting when we sang the hymn with the words projected onto screens on the huge stage; there was the text as I had written it and, alongside it, a translation into Spanish by Nanin Braulio of Puerto Rico, a member of the planning team. Several years after the hymn's first use, someone pointed out to me that since the hymn is addressed to God, the first stanza was grammatically incorrect. It read:

> God, who spins the whirling planets,
> Fills the seas and spreads the plain,
> Molds the mountains, fashions blossoms,
> Calls forth sunshine, wind, and rain—
>   We, created in your image,
>   Would a true reflection be
> Of your justice, grace, and mercy
>   And the truth that makes us free.

My friend the grammarian said, "It should either be 'God, who spin the whirling planets' (continuing with verb forms appropriate to 'you') or 'God, you spin the whirling planets.'" I had to admit that this had not occurred to me. The first solution seemed grating to the ear, and the second, though quite possible, could not easily be substituted in all the various places the hymn had been used by that time. I originally intended the first half of the first stanza to be a kind of ascription, praising God for the creation, and then in the second half to pick up our desire to reflect the image of God faithfully. Now, after some pondering, I have altered it for the sake of grammar. I trust it will not cause too much confusion.

(9) Creator God, Creating Still
Genesis 1 and 2; John 1:10–18; John 15:26

This hymn was the second one I wrote. It was a time of particular focus on language, language about God as well as language about people. It appeared in *Concern* magazine under the title "A Hymn to the Trinity." I had been bothered by the way in which some people seemed to use the traditional Trinitarian formula, "Father, Son, and Holy Spirit/Ghost," in such a narrow way that it limited God rather than enlarging one's understanding of the wonder and mystery of God. This hymn, speaking of the Triune God in terms of function rather than in terms of Persons, is meant to help us break out of that trap of thinking we know God by knowing formulas. This expansion of who God is, it seems to me, was basic to the evolution of the doctrine of the Trinity. Is it any more heretical to suggest new ways of expressing the fullness of God than to box God into a rigid formula? I think not!

(10) O God of Earth and Space
Genesis 1; Psalms 8, 23, 111, 148, 150

The good providence of God the Creator is central to my understanding of God, who God is and how God acts. Throughout scripture, and especially in the psalms of praise, there is recorded how marvelously God has provided what is needed for the human family. But I have an argument with the psalmists. Awe of God's providence should never be distorted into self-centered gratitude for what we have that someone else does not have. God's care is also a providence that extends beyond material things into the realm of the spirit, where God has just as wonderfully provided music, thought, art, faithfulness, love, and justice.

This hymn does not deal with our abuse of these gifts but instead is an outpouring of praise for the wonder of it all. Confession comes elsewhere! The choice of "Yigdal," a powerful Hebrew melody, underscores the deep-rootedness of God's providence in Judeo-Christian thought and tradition.

I had written these words not long before learning of the hymn competition being conducted by Trinity Lutheran Seminary in Columbus, Ohio, as part of its 150th anniversary celebration in 1981. I submitted the hymn, and to my delight it was awarded the prize for best original text.

(11) God Reigns O'er All the Earth!

In 1981 I was asked to write a hymn for the 200th anniversary celebration of Redstone Presbytery in Pennsylvania. Of three I wrote for their consideration, this was their choice. (The other two are included in the section on anniversaries and dedications, Nos. 49 and 50.)

In this hymn I like the progression of the awareness of God's reigning in our lives—in physical surroundings, in the various stages and ages of life, in time and space, and supremely in Christ, God with us.

Several pastors in rural areas of the United States have mentioned their special appreciation of these words. On the other hand, a city dweller once scolded me for "no mention of the city." I was forgiven when I pointed out that Redstone Presbytery is made up primarily of towns and countryside. And, after all, you cannot cover everything in every hymn!

(12) Designer, Creator, Most Provident God

This hymn was written in 1984 for the installation of Jean Anne Swope as the Director of Land's End, a conference center of the Synod of the Northeast, set far north on Saranac Lake in the Adirondacks. The hymn reflects the location and its natural beauty as well as its relative isolation, which contributes to its value for study, concentration, and challenge. Most of us find such places in our lives—if not in reality, surely in our dreams.

(13) Sing Praise and Hallelujah!

Glendeen Wiig, better known as Corky, the choir director from First Presbyterian Church in Bancroft, Nebraska, called to see if I would consider writing a special hymn for that congregation's centennial celebration in 1986. I asked for information about the church and received these marvelous notes from the hand of an eighty-eight-year-old member of the congregation.

Hallelujah! Hallelujah! For the Lord has blessed this church for 100 years.

It has taught the children to pray and sing and to tell the truth and trust the Lord.

It has married the youth and buried the dead and consoled the lonely and cheered the old.

Those who entered through its doors heard faith in God proclaimed to them.

All God's children were welcomed here: black and white and yellow and red. And all were taught to love thy neighbor as thyself.

Its rafters rang with joyous song on Christmas day and Easter morn.

From this humble caring church five men of God went forth to preach.

Through all the years within its walls eternal life it aimed to give.

> Merciful God, Holy Lord, we thank you for this lowly church and through the many years to come may Happy Birthday be sung. Hallelujah! Amen.

Corky added:

> In the very early years of our church we had quite a few Native American members. Notable among them were the LaFlesche sisters, Susette LaFlesche Tibbles (known as Bright Eyes), Rosalie LaFlesche Farley, and Marguerite LaFlesche. . . . The fourth sister, Dr. Susan LaFlesche Picotte, was the first medical missionary to the Nebraska Indians under the Board of National Missions of the Presbyterian Church in the Synod of Nebraska. . . . We had a Chinese minister for a number of years who spoke his first sermon in English from our pulpit.

The pastor at the time of the centennial celebration was Russell Tomlinson. What a heritage!

I had asked for suggestions of tunes that would be familiar so the congregation could sing with enthusiasm. George J. Webb's tune was, I thought, the most celebrative one suggested for singing Hallelujah!

(14) God of Wisdom, Truth, and Beauty
(15) Great God of All Wisdom, of Science and Art

The planning committee for the first National Ecumenical Convocation on the Church and Education inquired about the possibility of my writing a hymn for the occasion. As is frequently the case, I wrote two. There is perhaps some duplication of thought here, but in the years since their first use in the summer of 1984 both have proved appropriate, particularly for festive college occasions.

"God of wisdom, truth, and beauty" focuses on the God who is Author of all arts, sciences, disciplines, and truth. "Great God of all wisdom, of science and art" leads us into the ways our learning can be put to good use in the service of humanity.

I can remember my father responding to an accusation that education was elitist, saying, "Education should never separate people from one another. At its best, education is meant to build bridges of understanding between people of all kinds." These hymns reflect that conviction.

Another concern illustrated by these hymns is that educational institutions, especially those related to the church, are an important arena in which to begin to use inclusive language. Not many years ago people would speak of the "brotherhood of man" in such circles without blinking an eye; unfortunately, some still do. Here is a primary place to show how inclusive language can call us to even higher visions for the human community.

(16) Ours Is a Singing Faith!

Arthur Frackenpohl and I had had some previous correspondence about my hymns when I received a request from him to write a hymn for the 175th anniversary of the First Presbyterian Church, Potsdam, New York, where he has directed the music program. He would then compose music to fit the text, with an arrangement for congregational singing and an anthem for the choir. He had the good sense and courtesy to inquire several months in advance, so I put the idea on the back burner, and there it simmered awhile.

The history of the Potsdam church and other information they had sent contained many references to music in the life of that particular congregation. The phrase "ours is a singing faith" came to my mind, and I decided to work on it. That required a six-beat meter. Because I usually have a tune in mind when I write words, I looked for a meter beginning with six beats and chose "Terra Beata," "This is my Father's world," as a starting point.

"Ours is a singing faith" appears here with a new tune called "Sandstone" by Arthur Frackenpohl.

(17) O God of Vision
Joel 2:28–29; Acts 2; Genesis 9:12–17; 1 Corinthians 11:23–26

The theme for the 1982 National Meeting of United Presbyterian Women was "Nevertheless . . . the Promise." I remember a conversation with Betty Ann Riley, coordinator of the meeting, in which she couldn't contain her excitement about the developing plans. The stage of the Hall of Music at Purdue University, second in size only to Radio City Music Hall, was to feature a vast rainbow by Corita Kent—six broad slashes of color, a hint of the enormity of God's promised covenant, with two colors of the spectrum reversed as if to indicate the unexpectedness of God's intervention into human life.

When I learned of the theme and considered writing a hymn for the event, I realized I wanted music with a long, sweeping line that would illustrate the faithfulness of our covenant-keeping God. "Lobe den Herren" seemed perfectly suited to the expanse and yet the urgency I wanted. The final stanza, written with the closing communion service of the meeting in mind, is an affirmation of faith and a rededication of our lives in response to Christ's call. The first four stanzas are sometimes used without this last stanza as a more general hymn of praise.

On opening night at Purdue, the service began with the curtains closed. The more than five thousand people present sang this hymn for the first time, and as they came to the fourth stanza, "Break the sun's rays into color, a rainbow around us," the stage curtains parted, revealing Sister Corita's huge "Rainbow." It was a breathtaking moment.

GOD IN CHRIST

(18) O Promised One of Israel
(19) Is Every Time a Threshold Time?
(20) For Ages Women Hoped and Prayed
Matthew 1:17–23; Luke 1:26–55; Luke 2:1–20; John 1:1–5

These three hymns were written within the span of a few months when I was thinking about how the season of Advent, the beginning of the ecclesiastical year, is often underrepresented in hymnbooks. The wealth of Christmas music—hymns and carols, anthems and oratorios—overshadows the period just before the coming of the Messiah. Yet that time of waiting and wondering is just as characteristic of the Christian life as is the time of celebration. We still await the full advent of God's reign on earth, the overcoming of injustice, the feeding of the hungry, the coming of peace. The life and ministry of Jesus of Nazareth gave us a foretaste of God's reign, but we still live with the tension between "already" and "not yet."

Mary's Song, the Magnificat, is a treasure rediscovered in recent years, by ordinary students of the Bible, thanks in part to liberation theology and to others who help us read scripture with fresh eyes. That influence on my thinking is evident in these Advent hymns, although there is also reference to ancient prophecy.

(21) O Word Made Flesh and Come to Dwell
John 1:1–18; John 14:6–7

In the fall of 1980 a friend who thinks more scholastically and theologically than I do complained (or commented) that I had not written Christological hymns. This hymn and "Christ, of human life the model" (No. 37) were written partly in response to that challenge. Here is evidence that the reality of the Incarnation means more to me than the particular details of Jesus' birth. Emmanuel, "God with us," in that event and in our present lives is what is life-giving, life-changing, life-enriching.

"Melita" is an interesting tune, particularly in the harmony filled with accidentals in the last two lines. Its most familiar words are those of the Navy Hymn, "Eternal Father, strong to save." Perhaps because of that connection, there is a sense of the rolling sea, of the buoyant undergirding yet complex involvement of Christ in our lives.

(22) The Baby in a Manger Stall
Luke 2 and 24; Matthew 2 and 28:1–8

Of all times of the year, and particularly the Christian year, Christmas is a time for singing. Christmas carols are surely the most familiar of all hymns, and many people would know at least the first stanza of a dozen or more. So why write more? This is not an area of church hymnody that lacks material.

It is partly because Christmas *is* a singing time that we like to keep on singing in new ways. However, I discovered that I could not keep Jesus in the manger. For me, the wonder of Christmas, the awe of the Incarnation, does not stop with the newborn baby in Bethlehem. That baby grew up into a man, a real human being with challenges, frustrations, work to do, puzzling setbacks, an eventual cruel and violent death but a final and triumphant resurrection. So this "Christmas carol" leads us the whole journey: birth, life, death, and life again.

I especially like the way the sixth stanza ties Christmas and Easter, time and space, together in praise to God. I added this stanza at the end of another hymn (No. 36 in this book) written for the 1986 Youth Triennium of the Presbyterian Church (U.S.A.), because of its scope and usefulness as a choir or congregational introit or response.

(23) When Christ Is Born the Cosmos Sings
Luke 2:8–20

This Christmas carol celebrates all that Christ's coming means for those oppressed by hardship, poverty, injustice, or captivity of any kind. The "heavenly host" that brought the good news to the shepherds still interrupts our work and the frenetic busy-ness of the Christmas season. The great good news is that we are free "to be the best that we can be."

The hymn was written with "Vom Himmel Hoch" in mind as the tune. Our church organist and choir director suggested the sprightlier "Herr Jesu Christ." Its syncopated rhythm adds a joyful, bouncy quality instead of the legato, chorale style of "Vom Himmel Hoch." Whatever the tune, the tempo should be lively.

(24) God, Give Us Eyes and Hearts to See
(26) God, Whose Glory Reigns Eternal
(27) As Trees from Tiny Seeds Can Grow
Matthew 9:20–38; Matthew 13; Matthew 14:13–20; Matthew 27 and 28

These three hymns were written at a time when Jesus' parables were on my mind. I was also pondering the healing miracles as signs of the reign of God in human life. What does all that mean to us, living twenty centuries later but still confronted by that same teacher, storyteller, and healer?

"God, give us eyes and hearts to see" reminds us how much we fail to see and hear what is around us every day. Indeed, people with impaired sight or hearing often "see" or "hear" more accurately than those of us who assume our vision and hearing are flawless. Here is recognition that it is

God who gives us that more profound sight and hearing; and gifts from God, whether of sense or spirit, are cause for celebration and praise.

"God, whose glory reigns eternal" moves beyond the parables to the crucifixion and resurrection, the supreme story without which the other stories might well have been forgotten. "Beach Spring" is a haunting tune. It has a southern mountain flavor in its rhythm and harmony, well suited to this text.

"As trees from tiny seeds can grow" points to the hiddenness of God's reign in the midst of our daily experience. The language picks up the images of yeast, seeds, light, treasure, weeds and grain, and coins—all found in Jesus' parables. The hymn ends acknowledging that it is not we who find God, but God who seeks and finds us. That is the good news!

(25) Christ Jesus Knew a Wilderness
Luke 4:1–13; Matthew 26:31–35; Mark 14:12–15:27; John 19:16–30; Luke 22:14–20; Matthew 28:20; Hebrews 4:15

This hymn ties together the temptation of Jesus, as recorded early in the Synoptic Gospel accounts, with the events of the final hours leading up to the crucifixion. The theme grows out of my conviction that temptation was an ongoing experience for Jesus, not a once-for-all clearly delineated event. For me this is part of understanding Jesus as a fully human being, "tempted as we are, yet without sinning" (Heb. 4:15). It is the overcoming of the wilderness experiences throughout Jesus' life, culminating in a resurrection that overcame death—that most profound wilderness—which is redemptive for us.

(28) What Signs Has God Revealed to Us?
Matthew 13; John 4:7–26; Matthew 20:28

This hymn and others focus on Jesus' teaching and healing, death and resurrection as signs of the reign of God breaking into human life. Here is God showing us a radically different way to live and act.

The centuries-old English melody "Greensleeves," with its minor key combined with a lilting beat, adds to the sense of mystery yet joy we experience in Christ. There is an unfinished feeling about the end of the stanzas in this hymn, emphasized by the three-beat ending, unlike the two-beat ending to be found in "What Child is this?"

(29) Christ Calls Us Now, as Long Ago
Matthew 4:18–22; Mark 6:7–9; Matthew 28:16–20

This hymn was written with vocation and evangelism in mind. The sequence of Christ's calling us, sending us out, and walking with us is important for our sense not only that we are not alone but also that we are not the important actors in our witness. The language is contemporary and the emphasis is corporate rather than individual. Although the biblical references are direct, the phrases belong to today.

(30) Christ on the Cross Our Life Has Bought
Colossians 1:15–20; Matthew 27:45–56; Mark 15:33–41; Luke 23:44–49; John 19:23–30

Most of my hymns are hymns of praise in some form. I had not deliberately avoided the season of Lent and Holy Week; I simply had not sought a full range of hymnody. Then I was asked to be the speaker at a Lenten breakfast and decided that the special message I might bring could be a journey through the life of Jesus in hymns. This hymn was written for that program, and the format of singing our way through Jesus' life has been useful on several other occasions.

Friends have mentioned that this hymn helped them in times of sorrow because it does not deny the grief and pain or move too quickly into the resolution of sorrow.

The simple strength of "Quebec" contributes to the meaning of the text.

(31) Good News Is Ours to Tell!
Luke 24:1–11; John 3:16

I confess to a bit of mischief here. At the beginning, I had no idea how much a part of my life this activity of hymn-writing would become. In addition, particular hymns were the most distressing to those of us who were sensitive to exclusive language. Some people were experimenting quite successfully with new versions of familiar hymns, changing the exclusive language while trying to keep faith with the apparent intent of the original author. I decided to try another tack: to write whole new hymns using familiar tunes so they would be easily singable, and the tunes I started on were among those that bothered me the most.

"Festal Song" is the tune for "Rise up, O men of God." The mischief comes in choosing to use Luke's account of the first Easter as the basis for the hymn, since it is Luke who reports that the apostles did not believe the women returning from the empty tomb; their words seemed an idle tale. Hence:

> Good news is ours to tell!
> Let no one fail to hear!
> God gives us life; God conquers death!
> What's left for us to fear?

There is an interesting sequel to the story. I received a letter from a pastor in whose congregation there was a special ministry with the deaf. They asked permission to change the second line for their purposes to (as I recall) "It gives us faith and cheer." I granted the permission, even though my intent was to indicate stubborn refusal to hear, not a judgment on those with impaired hearing—who "hear" some things better than the rest of us. Perhaps the line should read "Let none refuse to hear!" In any case, the hymn is meant to say that the good news is for the whole world, even if women were the first evangelists!

(32) We Are a New Creation
2 Corinthians 5:17–18

My friend the Rev. Elizabeth Knott had been called to continue the work of organizing a new congregation in Altoona, Iowa. When the date for formal organization of the church, to be called the New Creation United Presbyterian Church, was announced, Liz wrote to ask if I would write a hymn for their chartering. "We are a new creation" is the result.

The hymn picks up on the excitement of new church development, the dreams for the future, and themes of justice and partnership in ministry and mission near and far away, as well as on the biblical theme of being, by God's grace in Jesus Christ, a new creation. The words have proven to be adaptable to many kinds of renewal and opportunities to begin again.

(33) Jesus Christ, Whose Passion Claims Us
(34) O Jesus Christ, Life of the Earth

Late in the summer of 1982 I received a letter from the World Council of Churches concerning hymns and other liturgical materials for the Sixth Assembly of the Council, which was to take place the following summer in Vancouver, British Columbia, Canada. The deadline for submitting suggestions had been extended slightly, but there was still a great urgency. The theme of the meeting was "Jesus Christ—The Life of the World." Several sub-themes and study materials helped to expand the overall theme. I wrote these two hymns within a couples of weeks.

"Jesus Christ, whose passion claims us" was sent in with "Hymn to Joy," by Beethoven, as the tune. In a few weeks a letter came from Geneva asking if I would select a tune of North American origin, since part of the purpose was to have words and music both of which were characteristic of a particular part of the world. In addition, Beethoven's melody from the Ninth Symphony was being used in a number of television commercials in Europe at that time and was therefore not received with enthusiasm as a hymn tune. They suggested "Lord, Revive Us" as one possibility, acknowledging that it did not have the power of "Hymn to Joy" but did have a distinctly North American sound. I tried it, liked it, and it appears here.

In "O Jesus Christ, Life of the earth" I wanted to use the words of the theme, making them applicable to the individual and corporate lives of people. The phrase "Jesus Christ—The Life of the World" does not easily fit a standard meter, so my solution was to begin each stanza with "O Jesus Christ" and end each with "Life of the World, and our Life!" "Mit Freuden zart" has an unusual meter and is obviously not a North American tune, but given the short deadline and no negative connotations, it held as the tune for the hymn.

(35) Christ's Word to Us Is Like a Burning Fire
(36) We Come as Kindling for the Fire
Luke 24:30–32

The Worship Committee for the summer 1986 Youth Triennium of the Presbyterian Church (U.S.A.) wrote me in October 1985 about the possibility of writing a hymn on the event's theme, "Like a Burning Fire." It was an enthusiastic letter full of information about the work of the planning committee up to that point and including outlines of each day's sub-theme as it expanded the overall theme of the event. The story of the Risen Christ on the road to Emmaus, "Wasn't it like a fire burning in us when he talked to us?" (Luke 24:32, TEV) was the key to the theme. They were interested not only in a theme hymn but also in suggestions for additional songs dealing with the daily themes. Their careful planning captured my imagination.

"Christ's word to us is like a burning fire" was written as the main theme hymn. I chose "National Hymn" as the tune, partly because I thought the trumpets introducing each stanza and interspersed throughout would be exciting and celebrative. Also, the long line of the meter (10 10 10 10) offers an opportunity to say more than in shorter lines and has a building energy.

For the suggested daily sub-themes for the meeting, I depended on "Tallis' Canon." The idea was to add a stanza each day, and the option of singing in canon had its appeal as well. The daily themes the committee had planned were:

Tuesday	"Kindling for the Fire"	Genesis 22:1–18
Wednesday	"Fire from the Lord"	Exodus 3:1–6
Thursday	"Through the Fire"	Isaiah 43:1–3 and Psalm 23
Friday	"Lighting Useless Fire"	Malachi 1:9–10
Saturday	"The Fire Burns Low"	Luke 24:13–24
Sunday	"The Promiser Keeps the Promise" or "Tongues of Fire"	Luke 24:25–35 and Acts 2

The sub-themes moved through Advent and Christmas, Lent and Good Friday, Holy Saturday, Easter, and Pentecost, indicating the direction of the planning committee at that time in their preparation. The seven stanzas for the six-day meeting were my response. The final stanza is the same as that for "The baby in a manger stall" (No. 22). In each case it summarizes the message of the hymn.

(37) Christ, of Human Life the Model
John 1:1–18; Philippians 2:5–11; Colossians 1:15–20

The Incarnation means more to me than the birth of the baby Jesus. Philippians 2, Colossians 1, and John 1 are Christmas stories as valid as the recounting of the shepherds' and the wise men's journeys to Bethlehem in response to their visions. Emmanuel, "God with us," is a mystery too profound for human understanding. Yet Christ has made that presence so real that the mystery becomes part of our praise.

Along with the awe in the mystery of God in Christ, this hymn also calls attention to many varied ways of addressing Christ. It is the wedding of immanence and transcendence that is the ultimate mystery.

THE CHURCH IN CELEBRATION

(38) On Pentecost They Gathered
Acts 2

This hymn is an example of one written to fill a gap in current hymnody. There are very few hymns about Pentecost, and yet that birthday of the church is of great significance in the ecclesiastical year. More hymns focus on the Holy Spirit, although even this Person of the Trinity is shortchanged, and many of the hymns concerning the activity of the Holy Spirit do not mention Pentecost.

This hymn picks up several strands of the account in the second chapter of the Acts of the Apostles, and there are more direct biblical references than is usual. The hymn ends with the hope that the celebration of the singular event that so empowered the early disciples that they went out across the known world to turn it upside down will inspire us to do the same in our day.

(39) O God, You Call, Create, and Lead

This is one of two hymns written in response to a request by friends for a new hymn for their child's baptism. The request came shortly after the birth of our eldest grandson and, as it turned out, the hymn was first sung during the service of baptism for our grandson, Peter Andrew Lowry, in Stone Presbyterian Church, Clinton, New York. I especially wanted to focus on the responsibility assumed by the congregation for the continuing nurture of children baptized into the church in their particular congregation.

The hymn may be adapted for baptism administered to adults by changing the last two lines of the first stanza and the pronouns from third to first person, so that it reads:

> O God, you call, create, and lead.
> Your plan provides for every need.
> We welcome all who come today.
> Make us your people here, we pray.
>
> Grant us a vision clear and free
> Of what our human life might be—
> Of loving service, gladly done,
> For great or small, for everyone.
>
> Call us to ministries of grace
> Fit for each age, each time, each place.
> Now in this sacrament we, too,
> Renew our covenant with you.
>
> Rekindle now our faith's small flame.
> Call us again each one by name.
> So may our faith burn bright ablaze
> To warm and lighten all our days.

(40) Wonder of Wonders, Here Revealed

This hymn includes two aspects I care about deeply: one is the fact that God loves each of us before we know how to love in return, and the second is that in baptism we become part of a worldwide family unbound by time or space.

Over the course of the next few years after writing these hymns I was to become aware that the sacraments are not well covered in Reformed hymnody. Perhaps in some periods of history, underemphasizing the sacraments was a reaction to what was seen as a Roman Catholic overemphasis on them. Today, with a renewed interest in both the depth of meaning and the manner of celebration of the sacraments, it is time for some new hymns—to say nothing of the expansion of ecumenical interest and activity to include Orthodox and Reformed dialogue.

(41) We Gather Round the Table Now
Mark 14; 1 Corinthians 11:23–26; Hebrews 12:1–2

This communion hymn was written with two particular things in mind: first, remembering the supper in the upper room and, second, celebrating World Communion Sunday and recalling all the "cloud of witnesses" and all the various occasions in which an individual Christian may have celebrated the supper.

The first stanza sets the scene with Christ as Host, Christ as the Bread and Cup, and Christ as the perfect Word Incarnate. It is quite possible to omit the two middle stanzas without losing the significance of this as a communion hymn. However, for use during Holy Week and especially for Maundy Thursday Communion, stanzas three and four are especially meaningful.

The hymn has sometimes been sung by a choir during the serving of the elements.

(42) Christ Is Our Unity
1 Corinthians 12:12–27

Jim Forkner, when he was Moderator of the Presbytery of John Calvin in Missouri, was trying to find a communion hymn that expressed the unity of the body of Christ and reconciliation within the human family that is one of the gifts of the Eucharist. He wrote to his fellow presbyter Keith Allison, asking if he might write a new communion hymn for the presbytery to express this unity. Jim noted in his letter to Keith that most communion hymns focus on the presence of Christ in the sacrament, Christ's body and blood, or perhaps on unity between the Christian and God or God in Christ rather than unity between human beings gathered together around the table. He wrote, "I need to discern the Presbytery member sitting in the same pew with me as being part of the body of Christ. I think the truth needs more singing!"

Keith composed this tune but could not find words that satisfied him, so he wrote to me, sending the tune and saying that they hoped to introduce the hymn during the communion service at the February 8, 1986, presbytery meeting some months away. These three stanzas came quickly to me and were submitted and accepted.

The tune is titled "Claudia." It is very singable, in an easy range, and easy to learn. I think it is a happy blend of tune and text.

(43) Greeted as Saints, We So Become
Romans 1:7; Romans 16; 1 Corinthians 1:1–3; 1 Corinthians 16

The editor of *These Days,* a daily devotional guide, invited me to write one day's worth of the November–December 1986 edition of the booklet, for All Saints' Day. I agreed and set the material aside for a while. When it came time to write the meditation, I decided to write a hymn for the holy day instead of the usual prose. The hymn reminds us that we are all called to be saints, set apart for whatever God-given task is ours in this day.

(44) God of Love and Joy and Laughter

Two very dear friends were to be married June 1, 1985. They asked me to write a hymn for their marriage service, and this is the result. At my request, they sent me some notes about what they did and did not want expressed in the hymn. Beethoven's "Hymn to Joy" was their choice of tune. That made it easy, because I seem to think in 87 87 D meter. They used the hymn as a processional, sung with enthusiasm and joy by the gathered congregation. Although written for a wedding, this hymn is also appropriate as a celebration of God's love, which knits together the whole human community.

(45) O God of All the Years of Life

In the year when our congregation was going to celebrate its twenty-second anniversary, Douglas E. Wagner was our choir director and organist. Doug was already a prolific composer of church music—anthems, responses, introits, descants, variations, arrangements for voices and for handbells. He asked if I would be interested in writing a hymn for the congregation which the choir might introduce on the Sunday nearest the anniversary. These words are actually a rewriting of a poem I had written several years earlier when my mother and I had presented a program for a women's association in a nearby church.

The tune, "Whitewater," is named for the Presbytery of Whitewater Valley in which our church, Saint Andrew, is located.

(46) Hear the Songs of Thanks We Raise

This hymn was written for the celebration of the thirty-fifth anniversary of the gift of the Gilmor Sloane House in Stony Point, New York, to the Presbyterian Church for use as a place where the understanding and support of the mission of the church would be emphasized and enlarged. The house is a key part of Stony Point Center, where meetings and activities in great variety are held. The stanzas of the hymn pick up some of the rich diversity of people and events that fill the center. A highlight of the summer each year is a Global Village, calling together an intergenerational, worldwide family. God does indeed "still richly bless this place."

(47) God, You Have Set Us in This Time and Place

A very dear friend, Mary Kuhns, was the associate pastor of the Church of Saint Andrew in Roswell, Georgia, touching the north side of Atlanta, at the time of the congregation's twenty-fifth anniversary. The building was being enlarged as part of the celebration of the anniversary. Mary asked if I would write a hymn for the dedication of the remodeled sanctuary and for the whole anniversary year. Her choice of tune was "National Hymn"; it was a favorite of hers and the trumpets would add a festive note.

The text incorporates several elements related to the occasion as well as descriptive of the life of that particular congregation. As it turned out, the hymn could appropriately be used in other such occasions of dedication or rededication.

(48) God, Creation's Great Designer
Genesis 1 and 2; 1 Kings 5 and 6

Carol and Dave McDonald, a clergy couple serving the church in Wabash, Indiana, inquired about the possibility of a hymn for the dedication of their church's rebuilding program. As an added incentive, Carol sent me a tune called "New Reformation," composed by her uncle, J. T. Morrow, in 1950 for a text by Roger K. Powell entitled "Lord, we thank thee for our brothers." The melody is singable and is in a standard 87 87 D meter, which worked out well.

It has been my style to try to write for more than a single occasion, even when a hymn has been specifically requested or commissioned. In keeping with that pattern, this hymn celebrates the skill and labor of human workers as well as of our creating God. The tune, though unfamiliar, is very easy to learn. The blend of text and tune may prove useful for other church dedications, or perhaps for Labor Day Sunday.

(49) Into These Hills and Valleys Long Ago
(50) We've Known Your Mercies, Lord

These two hymns, along with "God reigns o'er all the earth" (No. 11 in this book), were written in 1981 to be considered by the Presbytery of Redstone on the occasion of their bicentennial. Set among the hills and red stone banks of southwestern Pennsylvania, the area was once the mission frontier, and it is still primarily a town and country presbytery.

"Into these hills and valleys long ago" recalls our pioneer heritage of faith. Many of my hymns express the sense of being part of a church that spans time and space, unlimited by a particular geography or moment in history. However, having grown up in a small town and being aware of the many congregations in any branch of the church that are small in size and isolated by changing times, but nonetheless large in vision and in heart, I like to give those town and country churches new hymns to sing in praise of God.

"We've known your mercies, Lord" is a prayer hymn containing adoration, thanksgiving, confession, commitment. It is a corporate prayer but is also appropriate for personal private prayer.

THE CHURCH IN MISSION

(51) O Holy God, Whose Gracious Power Redeems Us
Matthew 28:16–20; Acts 1:8

This hymn was written early in my time of experimenting with new words for familiar tunes. For someone wanting to replace texts in which the language about people was exclusively masculine, "O brother man" was clearly a target.

I was serving on a synod committee dealing with mission interpretation and stewardship and was asked to try my hand at a hymn with a stewardship emphasis. I wrote three, of which this is one. If I were writing it now, I might do it differently. "Welwyn" is not the easiest tune to which to fit words. A clue to that fact is that the music often takes different forms or meters with the different stanzas. The difficult way to learn this is to print only the words and then neglect to inform the pianist which form works best. I finally settled on the arrangement that begins each line with a half note, even though some of the lines sound better with the emphasis on the second syllable rather than the first.

(52) Join Hearts and Voices
John 6:1–14

While serving as interim associate for Mission Funding for the Synod of Lincoln Trails, I had the opportunity to work with staff people from across the country who were similarly involved with mission funding concerns. I was asked to try my hand at a hymn dealing with the theme for 1983, "Multiply the Gift." This hymn was later printed on the back cover of the *1983 Mission Yearbook for Prayer and Study,* a rich source of information about the mission of the Presbyterian Church and sister churches around the world.

"Duke Street" is a favorite upbeat, singable tune. The combination makes a positive hymn of praise that focuses on gratitude as the basis for stewardship.

(53) O God, You Hear Our Every Prayer
Mark 12:41–44

Prayer, Partnership, and Peace were the announced themes of the Silver Anniversary of the Fellowship of the Least Coin in 1981. Hymns were written by people from all around the world; among them was this offering, a prayer for peace.

The Fellowship of the Least Coin began in the mind of Shanti Solomon of India. In the fall of 1956, she had not been permitted to go to Korea with a reconciliation team because of a visa difficulty. While she waited for the team in the Philippines, she prayed for a way to unite women worldwide in their concern for peace. Studying the story of the widow's mite, she thought how women everywhere—rich or poor, educated or illiterate, in cities or in the countryside—could pray for peace as each gave the least coin of her country each month. This worldwide prayer fellowship has grown to include women in every continent. The offering is used for special projects evaluated by the Asian Christian Women, through whom Shanti Solomon first introduced the idea. Each individual offering is tiny, and women are discouraged from giving more than their least coin in order to preserve the equal sharing of all. But the bonding of prayer is powerful, and the gifts multiply.

(54) What Surging Well of Joy Is This?
(55) Though Doubt Confronts Belief
Romans 8:31–39; Romans 15:13

"Abound in Hope" was the chosen stewardship theme for 1984 for the Presbyterian Church (U.S.A.), and an appeal was made for appropriate liturgical materials. Those who were preparing the promotional materials were concerned that "hope" not be watered down into an easy thing or sweetened into a pie-in-the-sky dream. It was to be hope in the midst of life's trials, hope when hope seems least likely.

"What surging well of joy is this?" is for those times when joy remains even in the midst of sorrow, when God's grace overcomes doubt and hope flies in the face of evil. The words lend themselves well to the quieter, simpler tunes in long meter. I chose "Rockingham Old" here, but the haunting plainsong of "Conditor Alme" or the calm assurance of "St. Crispin" (see No. 25) are good alternates.

"Though doubt confronts belief" acknowledges the reality of pain, doubt, and fear. The recurrence of the words of hope in spite of all that might occur to eradicate hope from our lives makes this hymn suited to times of trial and difficulty.

(59) The Peace of Mind That Christ Can Bring
(60) O God, to Whom We Sing
(61) O God of Justice, Hear Our Plea
John 14; Philippians 4:1–9

A second set of my hymns on the theme of peacemaking includes these three. They were written with the 1983 Peacemaking Resources in mind. Earlier hymns dealing with peacemaking dealt mostly with peace in the societal sense of peace among nations, peace with justice in public affairs, and peace as reconciliation between people or groups of people. There is also inner peace, or lack of it. There is the struggle for peace and the need to acknowledge our doubts, fears, and failures. No matter how lofty our intentions, we fail to achieve peace in any measure except by the grace of God. Recognizing God's initiative in all peacemaking efforts and confessing

our shortcomings, we can move with confidence in God's power to use us
as instruments for peace.

(62) Live Into Hope
Luke 4:16–20

I have described in the Introduction how the theme "Live Into Hope" was
chosen by the National Executive Committee of United Presbyterian
Women for the 1976 National Meeting to be held at Purdue University,
West Lafayette, Indiana, in July. The Bible study was the fourth chapter of
Luke, describing Jesus' return to Nazareth at the beginning of his ministry
and focusing on Jesus' reading from Isaiah 61:

> The Spirit of the Lord is upon me,
> because God has anointed me to preach good news to the poor,
> and has sent me to proclaim release to the captives
> and recovering of sight to those who are blind,
> to proclaim the acceptable year of the Lord.

The team working on worship and the integration of the whole program
searched for a hymn that expounded the theme, was written in inclusive
language, raised one's spirits (even while dealing with difficult issues), and
was familiar enough to be sung with enthusiasm from the beginning of the
meeting. The search floundered.

"Truro" has been a favorite tune of mine for many years, and the opening
notes fit "Live into hope" perfectly, so I sat down at my typewriter and
spun out twelve stanzas—later reduced to four—incorporating the theme
and sub-themes of the meeting. It was the first hymn I ever wrote. Little
did I realize I had found a new vocation!

(63) God of Justice, God of Mercy
(57) Let Justice Flow Like Streams
Micah 6:8; Amos 1–9

These hymns were written for two special events, both spotlighting
economic justice for women, sponsored by the seven women's groups of
the reuniting Presbyterian churches.

"Women Moving Together for Justice" was the theme of the Women's
Breakfast at the 1983 General Assembly in Atlanta, Georgia, the Assembly
reuniting two Presbyterian denominations that had been divided since the
War Between the States. A further moving together was the fact that the
seven women's groups of the two former churches were in the process of
planning a consultation on economic justice for women to be held in the
fall of 1984. Energy and interest were extraordinarily high and focused.

"God of justice, God of mercy" was written for the Women's Breakfast,
which took place just two days after the vote for reunion. The planning
committee chose an intriguing way to introduce the hymn: the stanzas were

used individually, separating the other segments of the program. This served to concentrate unusual attention on the emphases on justice as stewardship, empowerment, strength in diversity, economic and political justice, and vision for the future. The hymn has continued to be used, especially in connection with ministries of justice.

In contrast, "Let justice flow like streams" is short and to the point. It picks up several of the prophet Amos's illustrations and visions. Perhaps its brevity enhances the urgency of the issues of justice. The hymn was commissioned for the consultation on economic justice for women planned, supported, and sponsored by the seven women's constituencies of the reunited church. The book of Amos was the biblical basis; Washington, D.C., in the fall of a presidential election year was the setting. The idea for this consultation was initiated by racial-ethnic women who saw economic justice as it impacts on the lives of women and children as an issue around which all the women's groups could unite.

(64) God, Teach Us Peacemaking
(56) Great God, Whose Will Is Peace
(58) We Are Called to Be Peacemakers
Luke 2:8–14; Isaiah 2:3–4; Matthew 5:9; 1 Corinthians 1:23 and 25

In 1980 the General Assembly of The United Presbyterian Church U.S.A., during its meeting in Detroit, adopted the report "Peacemaking: The Believers' Calling" and made peacemaking a top mission priority of the church. A call went out for worship materials on the theme of peace and peacemaking. In response, I wrote three hymns that summer: "God, teach us peacemaking," "Great God, whose will is peace," and "We are called to be peacemakers."

The first is concerned about peacemaking in an individual's life at an immediate level rather than, for instance, the nuclear threat or peace among nations. The focus is on the inseparability of justice and peace and on various arenas of our lives in which peacemaking is applicable— church, home, school, politics, the workplace.

"Slane," a traditional Irish melody, would not be an easy tune were it not for the familiar words "Be Thou my Vision." I have been fond of that hymn for years, but there is the phrase in the second stanza, "Thou my great Father, I thy true son," that now makes me feel omitted, and "man's empty praise" in the third stanza is not the only empty praise a person might hear.

If memory serves me correctly, the fourth stanza of "Great God, whose will is peace" was the first I wrote. Someone once called my attention to the fact that it is the only stanza that does not address God, but rather people who are peacemakers. That is true, but I picture us, even in the midst of directing our thoughts and prayers to God, turning to the community of faith and exhorting each other to live out our commitment to peacemaking. So I let it stand.

The hymn was written with Ralph Vaughan Williams' tune "Sine Nomine" in mind, the familiar setting for "For all the saints who from their labors rest." Copyright permission was in question, so I asked my friend Douglas E. Wagner if he would be willing to compose a new tune. "Westfield" is his contribution.

The third of these hymns is "We are called to be peacemakers." One of its real advantages is that it has only three stanzas. I know now why the Wesleys could, and did, write dozens of stanzas to try to express *all* they wanted to say. It is a pernicious assumption that a writer has only one chance to say something!

On singing through this hymn the first time, my mother pointed out that the emphasis in the word "peacemakers" in the first line comes on a syllable different from the one we stress in normal speech. She was satisfied when I explained that that was my intention. We are indeed called to be peace*mak*ers, not just peace-*think*ers or peace-*pray*ers. I like the nerve of this hymn: "O, for Christ let us be fools!" For those who prefer a major key, "Hyfrydol" is an alternative tune.

(65) "Your Kingdom Come!" Great God, We Pray
Matthew 6:7–13

"Your Kingdom Come!" was to be the theme of the Pre-Assembly Conference on Mission held just before the 1982 General Assembly meeting in Hartford, Connecticut. I was asked to write a theme hymn to be sung to the tune "Old Hundredth," using the Ralph Vaughan Williams setting for choirs, congregation, brass, timpani, and organ. Further, the expansion of each sub-theme to be addressed in each stanza was outlined in considerable detail.

" 'Your kingdom come!' great God, we pray" was written at a time when I was especially trying to avoid gender-specific words in relation to God as well as the people of God, and "kingdom" was a borderline word in that context, biblical though it was. My way of dealing with the dilemma was to use "kingdom" in quotation marks in both places where it appears in the hymn, and to expand the meaning of "kingdom" beyond geographical connotations by other words such as "rule," "law," "will," and "plan." In other hymns I speak of the reign of God.

(66) Sing to Our God a Song of Cheer
Psalm 100

This is a hymn for churches particularly sensitive to persons with handicapping conditions. The first and last stanzas may be used as a complete hymn, or one or more of the middle stanzas may be included, as appropriate to the particular ministry. Stanza two deals with physical—that is, motor—handicaps, stanza three with sight, and stanza four with hearing. The hymn could be used in dedication of an adaptation of the church building to be more accessible for all people.

(67) Christ's Partners All Are We
Matthew 7:9; John 15:12–17

This is one of my earliest hymns, and it taught me a valuable lesson. The original version had a few too many syllables in some spots. Of course, *I* could make the words fit the music. The test came when a committee sang it and could *not* make the words fit easily. This reworked text is clearer and more decisive in its meter.

The hymn celebrates the mission of the church. It picks up some important current understandings of partnership and mutuality in mission, of giving and receiving, of teaching, healing, and doing justice, of forms of worship from around the world that enrich worship in other places. The joyful recurring "Alleluia! Amen!" of the tune, "Madrid," provides a wonderful affirmation of the church's mission.

Why is "Amen" absent from the end of the other hymns in this book? This is not an issue of inclusive language! (I was asked about this in a workshop once, and it was a great reassurance to the inquirer that "Amen" is not a sexist word.) Most hymnals being published today omit "Amen" at the end of the hymns for a variety of reasons:

> The practice of adding "Amen" was a relatively late (nineteenth-century) addition to church hymnody, so the omission is a return to authentic roots.

> Not all hymns are prayers or doxologies, for which "Amen" would be an appropriate ending.

> In some cases, the addition of a simple (dull?) "Amen" is an anticlimax after an uplifting ending.

> "Amen" as an affirmation is considered unnecessary, because the congregation has already affirmed the words by singing them.

(68) Called as Partners in Christ's Service
John 15:12–17; Galatians 6:2; Ephesians 2:14–22

This is the hymn for which I receive the most requests for permission to reprint the words. It was written for the Women's Breakfast at the General Assemblies of The United Presbyterian Church U.S.A. and the Presbyterian Church in the United States, held concurrently in Houston, Texas, in 1981, two years before the denominations reunited. The hymn was specifically directed at the idea of the partnership of women and men in the church. In the former UPCUSA there had been considerable celebration of the fiftieth anniversary (1980) of the ordination of women as elders and the twenty-fifth anniversary (1981) of the ordination of women to the ministry of word and sacrament. Those kinds of partnership in leadership were on my mind as well as the theme of the Women's Breakfast at General Assembly. However, in the intervening years, these words have taken on a life of their own as they have spoken to the partnership between clergy and laity, pastors and congregations, clergy couples, and others.

Requests come from seminary classes approaching graduation. Requests come from men and women as they plan their ordination services and installation services. Some have come from couples planning their marriage service, and certainly from clergy couples serving the same congregation.

The first version of this hymn was introduced to a meeting of the Council on Women and the Church on which I was serving. In the second stanza the line "Let us follow, never faltering" was "Let us follow, never tiring," which rhymed with "Christ's inspiring" and did not necessitate contracting a three-syllable word or two; but someone gently pointed out to me that we *do* get tired! I agree, and so the word was changed.

(70) The Call to Be God's People

My friend Suzanne Goodrich telephoned me soon after she received the call to be the Executive Presbyter of Homestead Presbytery in Nebraska to ask if I would write a hymn for her installation service, June 28, 1983. She was concerned to emphasize the partnership of all the people within the presbytery to accomplish the work of the church in that place. She wanted to tie her ministry as a laywoman, called to a vocation often filled by ministers of the word, with the past and the future as well as the present. This hymn speaks to and for all of us who are called to be God's people in our own way, in our own time and place.

(71) Called by Christ to Love Each Other
Acts 1 and 2; Matthew 13 and 5; 1 Peter 2:9–10

While working on an Education for Mission project, I was asked to write some possible hymns for use in consultations to be held across the United States. These conferences would have participants representing churches from all around the world and would highlight mutuality and partnership in the mission of the church universal.

When I wrote this hymn, using the tune "Vesper Hymn" attributed to Bortniansky, I stopped after the first repetition of the phrase "Follow Christ, not counting cost," and similarly in subsequent stanzas. However, when the planning committee sang it for the first time, someone suggested the additional repetition, as it is printed here. Either format is possible.

There is a strength, I think, in the persistent repetition that pushes the worshiper to pay attention to the words.

(72) Christ Has Called Us to New Visions
(69) O God, Whose Glory Shines Afar
Luke 18:9–14; Romans 8:18–25; Matthew 9:5–8; Amos 5:21–24

The committee working on the program for the National Council of Churches Ecumenical Event to be held in Cleveland, November 1981, sent me some tentative plans and asked if I would write a hymn for the occasion. Themes to be woven through the meeting were peace and reconciliation for survival, the dignity of the human family, the unity and diversity of the human family, a vision of the future, and renewal and commitment.

I wrote both these hymns in response; "Christ has called us to new visions" was chosen as the processional for the final worship service, brightened with brass and percussion and colorful banners. It has proved a useful hymn in Presbyterian circles in working toward reunion of the two denominations. It is also appropriate to ordination and installation services.

"O God, whose glory shines afar" is a simpler hymn of praise, also useful in a variety of services of worship.

(73) Great Creator God, You Call Us

With the reunion of the two former Presbyterian churches into the Presbyterian Church (U.S.A.) in 1983, the Articles of Agreement were set in motion. One provision was the establishment of a General Assembly Council, elected to serve for the first six years of the new denomination's life, 1983–1989. It was a body given weighty responsibilities, not least among them that of becoming a united council on behalf of the church. Several people had suggested that I write a hymn for the General Assembly Council, but it was the Rev. Kenneth Hall, the second Moderator of the Council, who kept urging me to do so, and during his year as Moderator I wrote this hymn.

Since then it has been sung at almost every meeting of the Council. It wears well. Different phrases seem to gain meaning as our work continues. Its message has broader application than just for the Council's life and work.

I did not choose Henry Smart's tune "Regent Square" by accident. One of the texts frequently sung to this tune is "Christ is made the sure Foundation, Christ the Head and Cornerstone." I count on those words also being sung subliminally when this new hymn text is sung, so that we never forget who is Head of the church. (Of course, "Angels, from the realms of glory" is another familiar text to this tune. The Council should *not* have that image of itself!)

Topical Index

Index
of Scriptural
Allusions

Index of Composers and Sources

Alphabetical Index of Tunes

Metrical Index
of Tunes

Index
of First Lines